·OR·PLAN·

/16" = 1:0"
ELEVATION

10 14 18 112 116 120 124 128 132 136 140 144 148 152 156 160 FEET
·SCALE·FOR·PLAN·T·ELEVATION·

NOTE:
FOLLOWING·ISSUE·OF·
THE·MONOGRAPH·SERIES·
WILL·CONTAIN·MEASURED·
DRAWINGS·OF·THE·INTERIOR·
OF·THE·BRICE·HOUSE·

NNETH CLARK.

·E V A T I O N · · N ·

·E · H O U S E ·

M A R Y L A N D ·

SPIRIT OF
NEW ENGLAND

Other National Historical Society Publications:

THE IMAGE OF WAR: 1861–1865

TOUCHED BY FIRE: A PHOTOGRAPHIC PORTRAIT OF THE CIVIL WAR

WAR OF THE REBELLION: OFFICIAL RECORDS
  OF THE UNION AND CONFEDERATE ARMIES

OFFICIAL RECORDS OF THE UNION AND CONFEDERATE NAVIES
  IN THE WAR OF THE REBELLION

HISTORICAL TIMES ILLUSTRATED ENCYCLOPEDIA OF THE CIVIL WAR

A TRAVELLER'S GUIDE TO GREAT BRITAIN SERIES

For information about National Historical Society Publications, write:
Historical Times, Inc., 2245 Kohn Road, Box 8200, Harrisburg, Pennsylvania 17105

SPIRIT OF NEW ENGLAND

From material originally published as
The Georgian Period
edited by
Professor William Rotch Ware

Lisa C. Mullins, Editor

Roy Underhill, Consultant

A Publication of
THE NATIONAL HISTORICAL SOCIETY

Library of Congress Cataloging-in-Publication Data

Spirit of New England
    (Architectural treasures of Early America; 16)
    1. Architecture, Colonial — New England.
2. Architecture — New England. I. Mullins, Lisa C.
II. Underhill, Roy. III. Series: Architectural
treasures of Early America (Harrisburg, Pa.); 16.
NA715.S65 1988   720'.974   88-17972
ISBN 0-918678-38-2

CONTENTS

TELL ME WHY

Whenever two students of early architecture get together, there are at least three opinions to fuel the burning question—*why?* Why did they round the ends of the shingles? Why is there an overhang at the second-floor level? Why? Why? Why? If only we could travel back in time and ask the builders themselves. Yet, so complex is the web of influences, the honest and thoughtful builder would probably have to answer, "I don't know, it's just the way you do it." Yet, centuries later, we who can barely grasp our own motivations feel quite at ease explaining the behavior of time-distant strangers.

The ready answers to the question *why* usually come from one of two schools. One school explains every joint and moulding as a reflection of the social order. This is the "impress the natives" thesis. The other school finds a technical, constructional function for every corner and curlicue. This is the "it helps the water run off" thesis. Certainly, though, we find better answers when we understand the considerations of both schools. Enduring work has both style and substance. It must make the appropriate social statements in a real world of decay, wind-loads, and generations of general knocking about.

Englishman Joseph Moxon illuminated both the practical and style-conscious aspects of window-frame construction in his 1678 *Mechanick Exercises.* "The square Corners of the Frame next the glass is Bevell'd away on both the out and inside of the Building, that the Light may the freelier play upon the Glass. And upon that Bevel is commonly Stuck a Molding (for Ornament sake) according to the Fancy of the Workman, but more generally according to the various Mode of the Times."

Moxon's successor, Richard Neve, found it easier to discern human foibles in design when he wrote of foreigners in his 1726 *Builder's Dictionary.* "In Italy, . . . they so contrive their Partitions, as when all the Doors are open on a Floor, one may see through the whole House, . . . This Custom I suppose to be grounded upon a fond Ambition of Displaying to Strangers all their Furniture at one View."

Thus begins the study of buildings as tools of social function. How is the social structure reflected and reinforced by this form? How does a house communicate status, both in its exterior view and in its interior spaces? Even in the communal space of the timber-framed medieval open hall with the master and servants sharing the central, chimneyless hearth, scholars have discovered hierarchies. The master kept his table at one end, and the builder always put the best side of the exposed beams facing into his end of the room. Natural resources also shape the way buildings communicate. Profligate use of wood in a building was an obvious way to demonstrate high status in timber-short England. Close-studded timber homes show where the rich people lived, wide-studded walls with broad wattle and daub panels made homes for everyone else. When you've got it—flaunt it.

American colonial homes generate a host of *why*'s. Why did they often round the bottoms of shingles, giving the roof a fish-scale pattern? Was it "just for looks," or does it "help the water run off"? The answer is—yes. It looks good and it also concentrates water at one point at the bottom of each shingle so that it drips off, dries out faster, and lasts longer. If it looked good but made the roof deteriorate, it probably wouldn't be done.

Often our question is not *why* they did it but *what* they did. When we have to guess, we can seldom avoid projecting our knowledge or our ignorance into previous centuries. At one early reconstruction of a seventeenth-century settlement, the designers of the timber-frame buildings knew that "they didn't use nails back then, they used wooden pegs." Unfamiliar with mortise and tenon joints, they simply toe-nailed their timbers together with one inch wooden dowels. They had unconsciously applied the methods of modern two-by-four carpentry to heavy timber construction, creating a marvelous *why* for centuries to come.

In Chapter 1, George Gardner asks *why*, but offers no explanation of the overhanging second story on the Porter House. He does propose that the greater overhang found on earlier buildings was "a convenient vantage-point for shooting Indians"—certainly an intense social function. In old England, however, overhangs (or jetties, as they call them) are common; Indian attacks, are not. Is the overhang intended to protect walls from the weather? Then why is it usually on one side alone? Is it to gain extra space in crowded cities? Then why do they do it in the countryside? Each answer generates another question. The overhang can only be appreciated when we stop asking questions and just look. Like so many features of early architecture, it simply makes a beautiful house.

ROY UNDERHILL
MASTER HOUSEWRIGHT
COLONIAL WILLIAMSBURG

Colonial Architecture
in Western Massachusetts

Text by
George Clarence Gardner
Originally published in 1901 as
Volume II of The Georgian Period

East Doorway
CHURCHILL HOUSE, NEWINGTON PARISH,
WETHERSFIELD, CONNECTICUT
Built about 1760 by Capt. Charles Churchill.

COLONIAL ARCHITECTURE IN WESTERN MASSACHUSETTS

IN 1636 a small body of our Puritan ancestors, finding the country in the immediate neighborhood of Boston too thickly settled, the best building lots already occupied or appropriated, and perhaps, too, the political and religious atmosphere a little trying, gathered together themselves and such of their possessions as could be carried upon pack-horses and set out for the western wilderness. Beyond the straggling settlement of Watertown, then called Newton, they plunged into an unknown country absolutely wild and trackless, save for an occasional Indian trail. They had learned by that time that there was little possibility of stumbling upon the northwest passage or of settling on the shore of the Pacific—though the charter of their colony granted them the right to do so—but beyond these general negative ideas, the tales of Indians, and the varying reports of their own hunters, they were as ignorant of their destination as the "Babes in the Wood."

After a time they reached the Connecticut Valley and there they dwelt, scattered up and down the river between Northampton and Wethersfield, Connecticut, building up during the remaining sixty years of the century a straggling line of towns nearly one hundred miles in length. The growth of these towns and villages was slow. The distance from their base of supplies was great, severe winters and the failure of crops, combined with the constant inroads of the Indians, retarded development and immigration. For many years there was only a bridle path to Boston, and all merchandise had to make the long and perilous voyage around Cape Cod, through the Sound and the equally long voyage up the Connecticut.

The first settlement in the Connecticut Valley in Massachusetts was made in Springfield in 1636 and having the start in years and numbers the town grew rapidly and soon distanced its neighbors, becoming at last the leading commercial center of the western part of the state. Around it Longmeadow, Agawam, West Springfield, Hadley, Westfield, Southampton and Northampton, Hatfield, Deerfield and towns still farther north were slowly settled; some by immigrants from the eastern part of the state, some by wise men from Connecticut who had prophetic instinct, and others by those Springfield men who after a few years found their native town becoming too crowded, and saw in the tributary valleys and rich upland pastures of the parent river the promise of more abundant reward for the same amount of labor.

Hardly had the first of these valley settlements been established when the Indians, for the first two or three years friendly, suddenly took arms against the settlers and the war for mutual extermination began, an interminable struggle, barbarous on both sides, and one which would have exhausted the strength and patience of any people save our forefathers. Says Holland in his *History of Western Massachusetts,* "From the first settlement at Springfield, until the Conquest of Canada in 1760, a series of one hundred and twenty-four years had passed away, and by far the larger part of this time the inhabitants of the territory embraced in old Hampshire had been exposed to the dangers, the

E. BLAKE HOUSE, 1760,
NATHANIEL ELY TAVERN, 1667

Detail of Pilaster Cap
COLTON HOUSE, LONGMEADOW

through all this, the towns grew slowly, though not steadily. Springfield was practically laid in ashes in 1675, Deerfield met the same fate twice, and a half-dozen of the other towns barely escaped; but, always, the inhabitants—when there were any left—went to work and built again. How Florence in the fourteenth and fifteenth centuries fighting Pope, Emperor, Duke, Free Company, friend and foe, burning and tearing down, visited by flood and famine, found time for the art and architecture which she has given to the world, and above all how she has preserved it, impresses every one who for the first time reads her history, and in this Connecticut Valley the wonder is not that there is so little Colonial architecture, but that there remains standing a single structure built before the eighteenth century. Well, there *are* very few left. Still, until the early part of the present century there were a good many, and it is the march of improvement rather than that of violent destruction that has carried them away.

There is little doubt that from 1665 to 1675 Nathaniel Ely of Springfield kept a tavern in that town; in fact, twice he was fined, once twelve pounds for selling four quarts of cider to Indians, and again forty shillings for not keeping his beer up to the standard strength; and this tavern of his still stands, hemmed-in by brick blocks—perhaps not in its original form, but, likely, very near it, for the earliest houses in this region had undoubtedly steep gable roofs, as this has still. The "Pyncheon Fort," built by the first John Pyncheon in 1660, which stood until 1831, had the same steep gables, if a wash drawing made by the Rev. W. B. O. Peabody, one of the early Unitarian ministers of Springfield, is correct. In Hadley, in 1700, it was voted that the new meeting house have a "flattish" roof. As this was a thirty-degree roof, it is reasonable to suppose that the majority of roofs already built were steeper.[1] Then, too, the use of thatch being common, a steep roof was a necessity and it would be strange if the steep roof did not remain in fashion after thatch was discarded. I say the use of thatch was common, for "thatchers," in common with "carpenters, joiners, bricklayers and sawyers," received in 1700 three shillings per day, according to Governor Hutchinson, and of Northfield it is recorded that in 1702 "the planters built small huts and covered them with thatch." This house of John Pyncheon's, however, was not thatched. It had shingles of oak, eighteen inches long and one inch thick, which cost twenty shillings per thousand. In 1667, by the by, this same J. Pyncheon sold pine boards of good quality at his Springfield sawmill at four shillings and six-pence per hundred feet.

fears, the toils and trials of Indian wars or border depredations. Children had been born, had grown up to manhood, and descended to old age, knowing little or nothing of peace and tranquility. Hundreds had been killed, and large numbers carried into captivity. Men, women and children had been butchered by scores. There is hardly a square acre, certainly not a square mile, in the Connecticut Valley, that has not been tracked by the flying feet of fear, resounded with the groan of the dying, drunk the blood of the dead, or served as the scene of toils made doubly toilsome by an apprehension of danger that never slept." And still,

[1] The ordinary steepness of the early pitch roofs is shown by such structures as the older portions of the Fairbanks House at Dedham, and the Narbonne House on Essex Street, Salem. — WARE

Detail of Front Door
SAMUEL COLTON HOUSE, LONGMEADOW

Besides the Ely Tavern in Springfield, I know of no seventeenth-century building in the Connecticut Valley which bears any great resemblance to its original form.[2] Early in the eighteenth century, however, labor and materials had become plentiful enough to afford larger and more substantial houses, and many of these, very slightly changed, if at all, stand now. As a general rule, they are nearly all of the same type, varying slightly on closer examination.

It is with this class and type of house that I suppose, rightly or wrongly, the general interest in "colonial" architecture begins. That is, it is in this first decade of the eighteenth century that certain houses began to display more or less applied ornament, designed, most of it, from a varyingly distinct recollection of the latest style in England (or perhaps Boston) interpreted in wood by local geniuses with what simple tools they possessed. In nearly all cases the result was bad, but I do not know that it is less interesting on that account. Take, for instance, the entrance of Samuel Colton's house in Longmeadow. The house was built about 1740. It is clear that the builder, the carpenter and architect, who were undoubtedly the same, designed and executed as carefully as might be the really elaborate work about the door; every moulding has been worked by hand; the frieze moulds, the flat dentils of the pediment cornice barely raised above the paneling, the raised and bevelled panels of the door, and the carefully drawn radial-lines between the door and the pilasters; while the carved capitals and the decorated rosette with its bunches of grapes attached, the latter being in cast-iron, bespeak a man with a feeling for the beautiful, his vision a little befogged, perhaps, but his intention good. In these pilaster-caps did the designer intend to represent as best he could Corinthian capitals, of which, no doubt, he had seen pictures? Surely, if he did, he must have been a direct descendant of those Lombard-Byzantine artists and sculptors of the eleventh century who wrought in North Italy six hundred years before.

I have remarked above that these houses remaining to us from the colonial period (I use the word colonial here in an historical sense) are all of the same type. The same may be said of the towns themselves. All of the colonial Connecticut Valley towns, with the single exception of Northampton, were laid out on the same plan; the single street, often over three hundred feet wide, with a "common" running through the center on which the church generally stood. On either side of the street stood the houses, always with eaves to the street; the lots on which they were placed were comparatively narrow, and behind the house, at right angles to the street, ran a straggling line of barns and out-houses—on one side of the street towards the river, which, in general, was a short half-mile or less away, on the other to the swamp or the foothills of the valley, where each family dwelling on the street had its pasture, its woodland or its grassland; and to this day the great majority of these towns are unchanged in their plans, many of the original "home lots" being still owned by the direct descendants of those to whom they were granted in the seventeenth century. In the little town of Deerfield, there are twelve of these estates, and the average age of the houses on them is about one hundred and forty-three years.

The house built in Hadley, by Samuel Porter, in 1713, is a good example of the better class of houses. The plan was a simple one: two rooms on the first floor, with the chimney and entry between them, the chimney being the larger; upstairs, four rooms. At the rear was a one-story addition, which long ago fell away, to be replaced by another.

Why on the front the second story overhangs the first by four or five inches, I do not know. I can find no constructional reason for it. It certainly could not have served, as did the greater overhang on earlier buildings, as a convenient vantage-point for shooting Indians, though the house was built in the darkest period of the French and Indian wars. The clapboards are split and shaved, with their edges moulded. The front door is practically a double door made up of the ordinary panel door backed by a batten door on the inside, the whole being three inches thick. Despite the scarcity of pine, of which the records of that time often complain, all the interior partitions are solid and paneled in wood, and there is paneled wainscot everywhere, the width of the panels testifying to the scant respect paid to that provision in the colonial charter which reserved all trees over twenty-four inches in diameter for the use of the Royal Navy. The extent of wood-paneling was brought to my notice by the present dweller in the house by the eminently practical observation that the room took forty yards of carpeting and only two double-rolls of wall paper. All of this detail, panels, mouldings, wainscot-caps, stair rails and balusters, is of the simplest sort, rather heavy and perhaps clumsy, but evidently local work. It is a significant fact that in the year that this house was built, the town meeting, of which this Samuel Porter was the moderator, voted to build its new meeting house, the one with the aforesaid "flattish" roof, and the committee voted to "buy glass, nails, and other necessaries, lay out work by getting clapboards, shingles, etc., hire workmen, improving our own inhabitants as

---

[2] While this may be true of the writer and, perhaps, of the Connecticut Valley, there are still left in many New England towns and villages a number of houses and other buildings erected in the last half of the seventeenth century still unchanged. — WARE

Front Door
STEBBINS HOUSE, DEERFIELD, MASSACHUSETTS
Built by Joseph Stebbins, 1772.

Rear Door
STEBBINS HOUSE, DEERFIELD, MASSACHUSETTS
Built by Joseph Stebbins, 1772.

Staircase in Hall
HOLLISTER HOUSE, GREENFIELD,
MASSACHUSETTS

much as may be, and levelling all the work at money price." Is it possible that the moderator may have found it convenient to build his house at the same time, and perhaps get a little better price on his own work? Such things have been done in later days.

There are a good many of these old houses very like the Porter House—in fact, almost identical with it in plan and detail—scattered up and down the valley. As the years of the century increased, the size of the houses increased also, and while the length of the house on the street was kept about the same, the two rooms on the first floor were increased to four, making the house much deeper. Then began to be built the gambrel-roof houses, of which the old Josiah Dwight House, still standing in Springfield, is as good an example, probably, as we have left to us. This was built about 1764 and outwardly is, in general, as it was one hundred and thirty years ago. There is a little more elaboration of detail about the windows and doors and the cornice, but the doorway is very like that of the Porter House in Hadley, like the Colton House in Longmeadow, and, in fact, like fifty other houses in the neighborhood. Here are the same wrought clapboards with their moulded edges, and the same pineapple in the center of the broken pediment above the doorway, the same indication of a flat arch above the door-opening, and almost exactly the same doors themselves. Inside, the house has been so completely torn to pieces and remodeled that only a few of the rooms retain their original shape, and instead of a score of representatives of one family, the representatives of scores of families, and possibly as many nationalities, now dwell there. Up to the close of the Revolutionary War this type of house, beginning with the narrower house, and gradually increasing in size with the change from the simple gable roof to the gambrel roof, seems to have been the prevailing plan all through this section of the country, and examples of it might be multiplied almost indefinitely, but it would amount to hardly more than a vain repetition. People were then, probably, pretty much the same as they are now: the recognized leader in a financial and social way built himself a house, and his friends and his enemies followed as closely as they could in his footsteps. Until the War of the Revolution, there was little, if any, diversity of opinion as to who these leaders were.

Of the distress occasioned by the War of the Revolution, the inhabitants of Western Massachusetts bore their full share, for though they were not exposed as were the dwellers on the coast to Great Britain's navy, and their comparative isolation and slight numbers secured them in a large degree from the more important movements and designs of the enemy, they made up a part of the frontier close to that debatable ground which witnessed the most bloody and barbarous conflicts in the struggle with the mother country, and the Indian allies of the British were a potent factor in their dread, for the generation was still living and active which had seen and felt the horrors of Indian warfare. The very strongholds which had been the colonists' defense, the trails and roads which they had opened, became, on the breaking out of the war, their greatest danger, and an enemy could strike from the depths of the forest about them more terribly than from the wide expanse of the Atlantic. With the fall of Burgoyne came some relief from immediate peril; but Canada still remained, a continual menace until the war had closed.

So it was that there was but little important building done here during the Revolution—at its close the country was exhausted, and Western Massachusetts bore its share of the general exhaustion. But though many fortunes had been lost, others had been gained: while the war crippled many industries, it built up nearly as many others, and many of these latter were exceedingly profitable ones, and the natural result of this state of affairs showed itself in the latter part of the eighteenth century in the building of many new houses, larger and more elaborate than any that had gone before; houses, too, which stood out from the majority in sharper lines of contrast to their neighbors, for until this opportunity presented itself for the accumulation of wealth, the money in these communities had been much more evenly divided. Then, too, the war had moved the people about geographically as well as socially; they had gone from the country to the city, and come from the city to the country, and so it was that new ideas and innovations were brought in.

Even before the Revolution, Boston and its vicinity had apparently had an "Art awakening"; the introduction to the *Town and Country Builders' Assistant,* published at a "shop near Boston Stone," by J. Norman, architect, seems to indicate a movement of this sort. He says in this "Introduction" to the volume of plates and texts, which he frankly remarks are "made familiar to the meanest capacity", "The greatest pleasure that Builders and workmen of all kinds have of late years taken in the Study of Architecture, and the great Advantages that have accrued to those for whom they have been employed, by having their Works executed in a much neater and more magnificent Manner than was ever done in this Country before, has been the real Motive that induced me to the Compiling of this Work for their future Improvement.

"Besides as the study of Architecture is truly delightful in all its Process, its practice is evidently of the greatest Importance to Artificers in general, and its Rules so easy as to be acquired at leisure Times, when the Business of Day is over by way of Diversion; Tis a Matter of very gret surprise to me how any Person dare presume to discourage others from the Study thereof, and render them very often less serviceable to the Public than so many Brutes. But to prevent this Infection from diffusing its poisonous effluvias any further, and in consideration that amongst all sorts of people there are some in whom nature has implanted that noble Faculty of the Soul called REASON WHEREBY WE JUDGE OF THINGS, I have therefore, at very great expense, compiled this Work for the common Good of all *Men of Reason,*" etc.

This "awakening," the Revolution, by its beforementioned shifting about, undoubtedly spread, and one of its results in this region was the publication at

HOLLISTER HOUSE—1797—GREENFIELD, MASSACHUSETTS

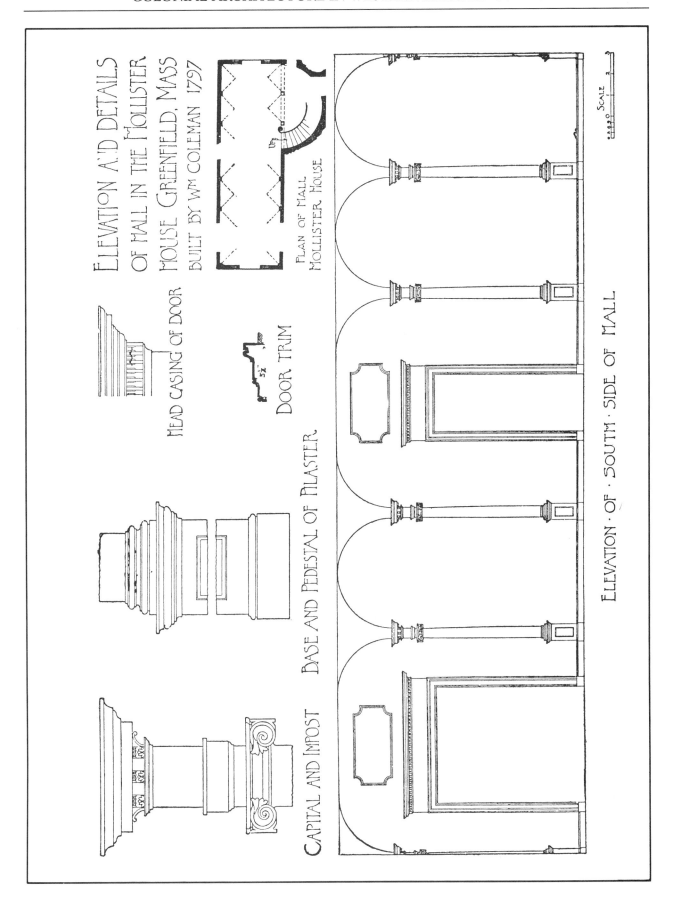

ELEVATION AND DETAILS
OF HALL IN THE HOLLISTER
HOUSE GREENFIELD, MASS
BUILT BY WM COLEMAN 1797

PLAN OF HALL
HOLLISTER HOUSE

HEAD CASING OF DOOR

DOOR TRIM

BASE AND PEDESTAL OF PILASTER

CAPITAL AND IMPOST

SCALE

ELEVATION · OF · SOUTH · SIDE · OF · HALL

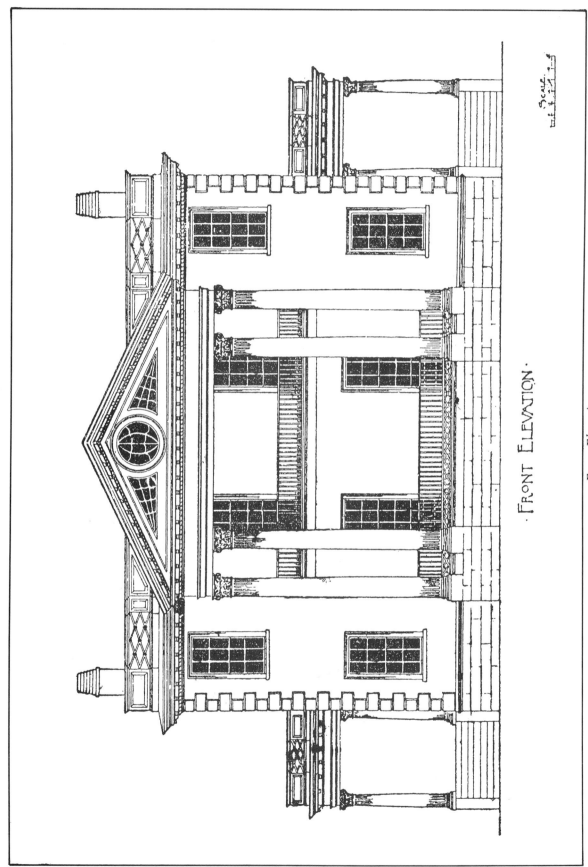

Front Elevation

ALEXANDER·HOUSE — 1811 —
SPRINGFIELD, MASSACHUSETTS

COLTON HOUSE — 1806 —
AGAWAM, MASSACHUSETTS

Second-Story Hall Capital and Impost
HOLLISTER HOUSE — 1797 —
GREENFIELD, MASSACHUSETTS

Greenfield, in 1797, of the *Country Builders' Assistant,* by Asher Benjamin. As nearly all of the existing "Colonial" work later than 1793 probably owes what it has of artistic merit either to this eminently practical little volume, or to the author — who was a carpenter — it deserves more than a passing mention. The book contains thirty copper-plates with a "Printed Explanation to each," which, taken all together, give a pretty thorough exposition of the construction and artistic detail of a house in those days. A half dozen of these plates I

have redrawn; for, intended as they were for working details, they are not without interest.

Plate 1 is mainly of door and window trim, which the author states should be $\frac{1}{7}$ or $\frac{1}{8}$ of the width of the door or window. The frieze over the door or window should be $\frac{1}{4}$ wider than the trim and the cornice $\frac{4}{5}$ or $\frac{5}{6}$ of the trim.

Plate II shows "Ionic and Corinthian Fronts . . . with all their parts figured for practice which is plain to inspection."

Plate 14 "is a group of cornices, and to proportion them to rooms or any other place required, divide the whole height of the room in twenty-two, twenty-four, or twenty-six parts, and give one of those to the cornice. . . . If used on the outside of buildings, divide the height into nineteen or twenty parts, one of which will be the height of the cornice."

Plates 15 and 16 show pedestals and imposts, the proper depth of the latter being $\frac{1}{19}$ or $\frac{1}{20}$ of the height from the floor to the springing of the arch, while Plates 19 and 20 are chimney-pieces drawn to scale with their details "half size." Of the remaining plates in the book, eight are devoted to the explanation of the orders; there are one or two plans and elevations of houses and a church, details of staircases, doors, windows, etc.; in fact, all that an intelligent builder a century ago really needed.

Of the earlier books printed about this time, some earlier, some later, *Builders' Jewels, Gentlemen's and Builders' Repositories, Builders' Companions* — I know of none that approach as closely the Colonial spirit, as it is embodied in this region, as Benjamin's little book. His plates are poorly done, but here is the translation of the Classic into the vernacular — Jones and Wren adapted to the necessities of pastoral New England.

Just about the time that Benjamin published this book, he built for Mr. Samuel Coleman, of Worcester, the house in Greenfield now owned by Mr. Hollister. It is one of the best examples of the work of its time in this part of the state. Coleman failed before the house was done (let us hope that the architect was not one of the causes of the failure), and the house was finished by the creditors. Their economy is manifested in the house by the hanging of $\frac{7}{8}''$ doors in frames that are rebated for $1\frac{1}{4}''$ doors. The building is nearly square with two large rooms on either side of the central hall, which runs directly through the house, having at the rear end a wide door, a counterpart of the front door, which opened onto the lawn and garden at the back end. The kitchens, pantries and serving-rooms were all contained in an L at the rear, which was built at the same time as the original house. The hall, with its coved ceiling cut by semicircular arches which are carried by delicate Ionic pilasters, is a very satisfactory piece of work, and the finish in each of the first-story rooms and nearly all of the chambers is evidently carefully studied for each individual room. The forerunner of the ventilating grate is foreshadowed in the fireplaces of the two parlors where the stone facings are perforated to admit the hot air from the room that the rooms above may benefit thereby. The house has passed through many vicissitudes, but is substantially now as the sketch shows, excepting that a front porch has been added which is omitted in the sketch, and which detracts as little as possible from the beauty of the original. It must have been thoroughly well built, for there is hardly a settlement or crack in the whole building.

The house built by Rufus Colton at Agawam in 1806 might have been inspired by this Hollister House so far as its front is concerned, and it is plainly an imitation of some other house. As the owner built it on the strength of a $5 lottery-ticket which drew him a prize of $5,000, and had spent a good deal of his prize before he began to build, it is safe to assume that it is a much cheaper house than the foregoing. These two houses are the type in general of the later Colonial work in Western Massachusetts. There are some of the large, square, gable- and gambrel-roofed houses, but they are all like the ones built earlier, except that their front entrances nearly all resemble the ones which Benjamin shows in his little book, instead of the heavy broken-top pediments like that in the Colton House at Longmeadow. The flat-hipped roof was evidently the fashionable roof in those days.

In 1811 was built the Alexander House in Springfield, and this house marks the beginning of the Greek Revival, in this part of the country at least. Here again, Asher Benjamin was the architect, and he seems to have spent some part of his time since he built the Greenfield house in the study of Greek work. All the curves in his mouldings about the house, inside and out, are Greek, and the acanthus leaves in the composite capitals have become sharp and spiky; he has grown artificial, too, for clapboards on the outside no longer content him for his façade. It is now smoothly covered with matched boards; his balusters have disappeared and slender straight sticks, geometrically arranged, have taken their place. The interior of the house shows these changes, too, for the trim throughout is like that which became common fifteen or twenty years later—a flat single member with five beads and imitation corner-blocks, with a small rosette in the center, though this trim, unlike later work, is still mitred.

There are a half-dozen houses still scattered about Springfield built from five to fifteen years later than this one, and evidently more or less copied from it, which show that this set the fashion, for a time, for the rest of

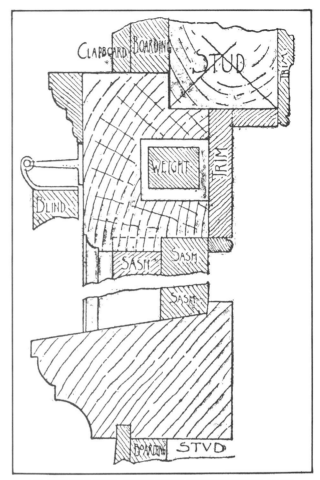

EIGHTEENTH-CENTURY WINDOWFRAME

the town. But with this house—possibly indeed with the type illustrated in the Greenfield and Agawam houses, the Colonial architecture, so far as it has any individuality, ends. After this time the misuse of the materials of which the houses were built became so apparent and so great that the later work is merely interesting as a thing to be avoided.

The earlier work is not always constructed on the best scientific principles nor with a view to special economy of materials and labor, as the little sketch of an eighteenth-century windowframe indicates, but it is far more logical in many ways and certainly better architecture than the later work—at least so far as wooden construction went, and wood was almost exclusively used in this part of the country. Of brick buildings erected before the early 1820's in this locality, there are almost none. Fortunately much of this later Colonial work has been thoroughly well preserved and the houses illustrated stand much as they were when they were built. The additions which were made to them forty or fifty years ago have been taken away, and there has been very little cutting of new windows and putting up of new partitions, with the attendant barbari-

FIRST CHURCH — 1702 — WEST SPRINGFIELD,
MASSACHUSETTS

ties of new doors and window-trim, which so often dis-
figure the houses of that period.

Far be it from me to claim for my forefathers who
dwelt in these western hills and valleys greater zeal in
religion than possessed the souls of their brethren nearer
the coast, but the proportion of white spires and belfries
to pilastered mansions and gambrel-roofed houses is
greater, I dare maintain, in Franklin and Hampshire than
in Essex or Middlesex counties, account for it as you will.
To provide a shelter for himself and his family was, of
course, from stern necessity, the first duty of the colonist.
But this was but an incident; no sooner had he a roof over
his head than he turned to his real and abiding work,
that combined civil and ecclesiastical structure — the

"meeting house." Indeed, in some instances, the church
proved the occasion for the town rather than the town for
the church.

This is not the place for a discussion of colonial history:
suffice it to say, that never, in modern times, has the
connection between Church and State been more complete and intimate than in the earlier colonial days of
Western New England, and that probably the ratio *per
capita* of politics and religion to the population has never
been equaled. The colonists had, most of them, left the
old country because they were unable there to be as active
as they wished in these pursuits, and they made the most
of their opportunities when they had the chance. So they
built their meeting house at the first possible opportu-

CHURCH — 1812 — ASHFIELD, MASSACHUSETTS

FIRST CHURCH—1750—
FARMINGTON, CONNECTICUT

in Massachusetts, was 18' x 26' built of squared logs, with a thatched roof, 9 feet high from the lower part of the sill to the upper part of the "rasens," and the builders were to be paid £14 in work or corn for its completion.

The first church at West Springfield, built in 1702 and torn down in 1820, was 40 feet square. There is a cut of it in *Barber's Historical Collection* which I have re-drawn. John Allys, of Hatfield, was the architect, and, for its day, it was a very pretentious church, its extreme height being 92 feet, and its topmost point surmounted by a large sheet-iron weather vane, with the date of its erection cut in it, over which a copper weathercock swung. The first church at Hatfield, built in 1668, was 30 feet square. The reason for building this last church—because the dwellers across the Connecticut found that the worry of leaving their homes on that side unprotected on Sunday distracted their attention from the services—throws a grim and significant light on the times. The first church at Deerfield was "of the bigness of Hatfield House," and the first church at Springfield was a square one. These earlier churches were almost always built in the center of the long, wide street, and were entered from at least three sides and sometimes four.

From the ground dimensions given above, it is probable that nearly all had, like the West Springfield church, steep hipped roofs, and the records in many instances state that these roofs were "thatched," but with what material is not quite clear.

In the next generation of churches, the square form disappeared and, as a natural consequence, the gable roof replaced the hip. The church was moved, in many cases, from the center of the street into line with the dwellings on one side, and then the tower at the front appeared. Of this type of church, I know none better than the one still standing at Farmington, Connecticut, so near the Massachusetts line that it may be included here. The general plan of the church is still nearly square, the pulpit being on the long side of the church and the galleries continuing about three sides. There are three entrances, one in the tower, one at the opposite end and one on the side opposite the pulpit. The body of this church is absolutely plain save for the entrances, which have "fronts" like the older houses throughout the region. The tower is very simple too, but as it rises from among the surrounding elms it is very beautiful. The slender spire is carried by the eight columns which rise from the belfry deck, and has been so firmly tied to them that 150 years of New England wind and storm have only succeeded in moving the whole tower four inches out of plumb. These same slender posts run down into the main body of the tower for at least twenty-five feet, braced and mortised, and pinned and strapped together while the tower itself is anchored to the main body of the church by oak beams, 14 inches square, which run completely

nity, and not content, quarrelled on doctrinal points, divided their parishes and built again—hardly waited to get comfortable homes in one town before they emigrated to the more remote wilderness and built a fresh meeting house, or held town meetings and voted to tear down the existing structure and build a new and larger one more befitting the needs and dignity of the town.

As a result of all this activity in the past, there are few ecclesiastical structures standing now of an earlier date than the first of the century, and it is to the town and parish records, which, in nearly all cases, are one and the same, that one must turn for any trace of the oldest meeting houses.

According to the above authority, the first church at Northampton, the second, by-the-by, west of Lancaster, through the tower and nearly half way through the church. Investigation of the construction of the spire itself is an object-lesson in the thoroughness and care with which some, at least, of our forefathers did their work. Every stick of timber is marked at either end and the corresponding mark appears on the stick which joins it. Even the edges of the nail-holes in the wrought iron straps and the heads of the clumsy hand-wrought nails are marked, so that the right nail should be without mishap driven into the right hole.

But this church is exceptionally well built, even the ridgepole has only a sag of 1½ inches in the whole length of the church. Nearly one-half of the shingles and nearly all the clapboards now on the church were put there when the church was built, and the successive generations of white paint in some places have made a covering nearly ⅜ of an inch thick. The frame is, of course, of oak. The central pole of the spire is a single white-pine stick and all the timber is hewn. The church was built about 1750, and is similar to the one at Wethersfield, Connecticut.

Although, chronologically speaking, the present church at West Springfield can hardly be classed with the one at Farmington, it is not far removed from it in its general character; but the form has undergone some slight changes in that it is longer and narrower, and that the three entrances are all at the front. There is very little of interest in the main body of this church and the spire here is very like the one at Farmington—a little more elaborate in its design; similar, but hardly so good in its proportions. The bell in the tower was re-cast from the one that was in the old building. The church was built in 1802, and up to that year the parish had used uninterruptedly the first church mentioned above, a period of 100 years, and the present one bids fair to complete its own century of life.

In the little town of Ashfield, in 1812, was built the church which now does service as a town hall. It was built by John Ames, of the neighboring town of Buckland, and is said to have been a copy of the church in Northboro' which Ames built there. He committed suicide before the church was completed, rumor says, because he feared he was going to lose money on the contract. The church stood, originally, at the top of a very long and steep hill, nearly half a mile from its present location, and was moved bodily, spire and all, to the main street of the village.

Here there is a change from the earlier type noticeable in the spire, the tall and slender form having given place to the double-curved turret. The former shape seems to have been abandoned after 1800, and the more elaborate Renaissance tower takes its place.

I have re-drawn another plate from Benjamin's book which seems to have some bearing on this Ashfield

FIRST CHURCH—1802—
WEST SPRINGFIELD, MASSACHUSETTS

church. The church which he illustrates suggests the one in Ashfield, both as to the design of the body of the church and the spire, so that it is possible that local authorities may be mistaken in assigning the design of the church to the Northboro' one.

Just about this time there was the same break in the Colonial work in this region in respect to the churches

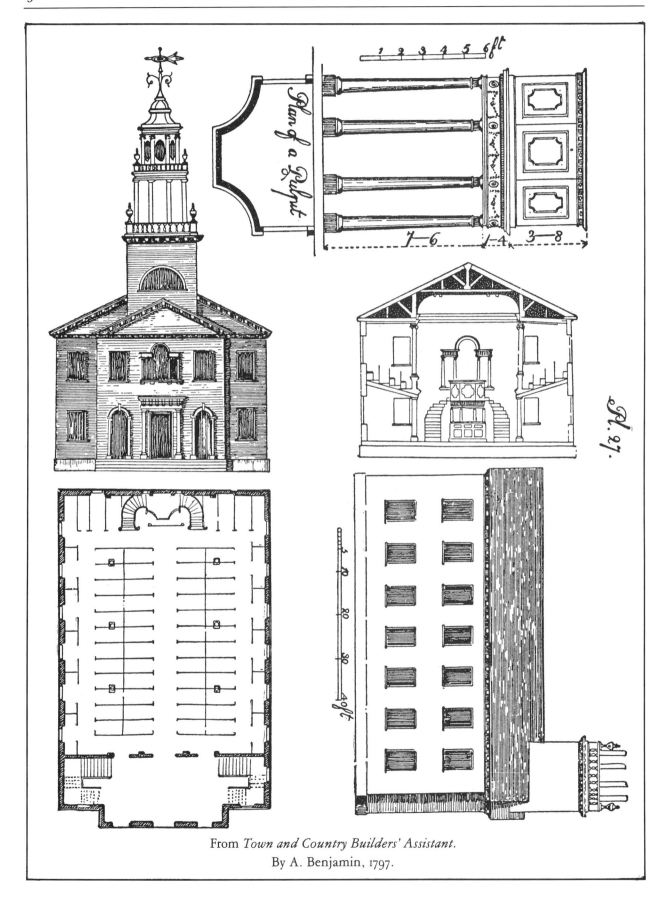

From *Town and Country Builders' Assistant.*
By A. Benjamin, 1797.

FIRST CHURCH — 1812 — NORTHAMPTON,
MASSACHUSETTS

FIRST CHURCH — 1818 — SPRINGFIELD,
MASSACHUSETTS

that occurs in domestic work, that is, the transition from the good work to the work which, while it is not distinctly bad, is not so good.

The three churches already mentioned make a reasonable use of the materials of which they are built. The wood mouldings, casings, architraves and pilasters are none of them wide enough to be unsubstantial, and are generally constructed with some appreciation of the fitness of things, but from this time on, more attention was paid to "correctness of style," I suppose, than to the legitimate use of materials.

The First Church of Northampton, begun in 1811 and finished in 1812, illustrates this very strikingly. It was designed and built by Captain Isaac Damon, a young man of twenty-eight, and was his first independent work. He had studied architecture with Ithiel Towne, of New York, and came to Northampton from that city to make the plans and direct the work. This church was undoubtedly the most elaborate of any which had been built in Western Massachusetts, and I know of none anywhere in the state which surpassed it. It was a large church, holding 2,000 people, and was in thoroughly good repair in 1878, when it was burned. The church which it replaced, from the description which remains, must have been similar to that at Farmington, and on the completion of the new building, the following advertisement was published concerning the old church:—

A BARGAIN.

The subscribers, being a Committee duly authorized for that purpose, offer for sale the

MEETING HOUSE

now occupied as a place of Public Worship in Northampton. The frame is perfectly sound and firm, and many of the materials of which it is composed are as good as new. Any Town or Religious Society in the vicinity that may be in want of a good and commodious House of Worship, will find it much for their interest to call and examine this building. Its dimensions are 70' x 48'.

In various parts of the Country, Meeting Houses have been taken down and removed a considerable distance, and thereby an immense expense been saved to the purchasers. A gentleman well acquainted with this business, who is furnished with all the machinery necessary for this purpose, is now employed on the New Meeting House in this town, and may be conversed with, and, if necessary, may be engaged to accomplish the object. It will be ready for delivery as soon as the new Meeting House is completed, which will probably be by the first of November

next. For terms, which will be found very easy and advantageous, apply to

JOSEPH COOK,
ABNER HUNT,
OLIVER POMEROY,
Committee.

NORTHAMPTON, January 8, 1812.

But no society seemed to care for a church at that time, so that eventually the old church was destroyed.

In 1818, the First Parish in Springfield appointed a building-committee to procure plans for a church having "a decent plain front," and appropriated $15,000, together with what the old church would bring, for the building thereof. This appointment resulted in the engagement of Captain Damon to build the meeting house still standing on Court Square in Springfield, a building, perhaps, less interesting as well as smaller than its Northampton neighbor, but with an exceedingly good tower. The church is still used by the First Parish of Springfield, and it is fortunate that no attempts have been made to improve it externally during the last seventy years, except for an occasional coat of paint and a re-gilding of the mammoth rooster at the top.

In Lenox, in 1814, a new meeting house was built of the same general type as these later buildings, the main difference being in the arrangement of minor details and belfry, and in the same town, in 1813, the county court house was built. This is one of the very few brick buildings having any pretension to architectural design left to us. This, again, was designed and built by Capt. Isaac Damon, who spent a year in Lenox on the work. Among other very interesting papers which are now in the possession of Mrs. Smith, of Northampton, Captain Damon's daughter, is a drawing of this Lenox Court House, which in its comparison with the building as it stands today, is interesting. Evidently, this was a preliminary sketch, for there were several changes made in the details of the building. The cupola is elaborated, the balustrade upon the roof is changed, and there are several other points of difference. The filling-in of one of the windows and the changing of the first-story window to a door were not contemplated on the original plan, but are later work.

Capt. Isaac Damon appears to have been the leading architect of Western Massachusetts from 1812 to 1840, his influence on public and ecclesiastical work being even greater than Benjamin's on domestic. He designed and built at least thirteen churches in this region and nearly all the town halls and court houses; his specialty, however, was bridges, and there are

CHURCH — 1814 — LENOX, MASSACHUSETTS

eral design and is a very late example of this "transitional" style, for most of the churches built as late as this (1826) were much more like the annexed elevation of Captain Damon's work.

The churches which have been mentioned above, like the houses on earlier pages, I have chosen as being types which illustrate the changing phases of our Colonial work. There are other houses and buildings which have more historic interest, others that are conspicuous through some strongly marked peculiarities, for there were architectural "freaks" one hundred years ago as there are today; but these have no connection with the general development and it is only with that that I have attempted to deal.

The bits of history which appear from time to time in connection with the building of meeting house or schoolhouse often have a more than local interest. The following old contract for the meeting house in Charlemont, dated 1762, shows that contractors, even in those days, were apt to be dilatory in the completion of their work.

"Know all men by these presents, that I Thomas Dick of Pelham in the County of Hampshire, Innholder, for and in consideration of . . . do by these presents covenant and agree to set up a frame in said town in the place where the old frame now stands it being 35' x 30' and 18' posts. To cover the outside with chamfered boards and the roof with boards and shingles and to put up weather boards. To lay the lower floor with boards and sleepers or joist well supported and to complete the same workmanlike by the last day of September next. Otherwise on failure thereof to pay said Treasurer 26*d*. for use of said proprietors.

Signed, THOMAS DICK

N. B. The proprietors to find boards, nails, shingles and rum for the raising." — June, 1762.

All through the old records and town histories these contracts occur, and however slight and brief the specification may be, the appropriation of — gallons of rum or cider for the "raising" is ubiquitous. That and the location of the church seemed to engross the minds of the worthy inhabitants, the former item having apparently unanimous approval, the latter being a most grievous matter of strife and contention.

The towns of Granby and South Hadley "split" on this account. In the little town of Cummington four or five meeting houses were built in as many parts of the town, to be abandoned, one after another, and in Southampton the town quarrelled for six years after voting to build, before the site was decided upon. But these matters only pertain to the architectural so far as

several of his drawings still preserved — rendered in a manner that indicates a most thorough training in draughtsmanship — of the old-fashioned bow-string truss wooden bridges. And of the bridges themselves there are still more left: nearly all those over the Connecticut from Charlestown, New Hampshire, to Connecticut, a half dozen across the Penobscot, others over the Hudson, the Mohawk and the Ohio — in all, a quarter of a hundred were built by him, and a large number of them are still in use.

This elevation of a church is re-drawn from one of his original drawings; where this particular church was built — if, in fact it was built at all — I do not know. It resembles closely any one of a half dozen churches erected in Hampshire and Hampden counties between 1820 and 1840.

The Congregational Church at Ware, though a little later, is strikingly like the preceding churches in gen-

COURT HOUSE — 1813 — LENOX,
MASSACHUSETTS

FIRST CHURCH—1826—WARE,
MASSACHUSETTS

A DESIGN BY ISAAC DAMON

they illustrate the thoroughness with which our fore-fathers grasped the subject in which they were interested, and the careful manner in which they studied and considered the main points of detail; and these characteristics they embodied in the buildings which they erected, buildings in which the construction and material must in many cases have been experimental, but which stand today monuments to the soundness of their judgment.

THE VILLAGE STREET

The plan of the early New England village which has often perplexed inquirers is purely a thing of natural growth. The necessities of mutual defense and the needs of social intercourse required that the earliest houses should be grouped closely together, probably without any common or definite grouping. But, later, when one early settlement was connected with another by a more or less well-defined path or road, it was only natural that smaller settlements should grow up between distant points and, naturally, the new houses again were built near together, but this time upon either side of the established roadway. The planting of elm or maple trees along the road, the wider separation of the rows of houses so as to include a common or green between them followed as a natural development and when the general scheme had reached this stage it was natural that the church and town house should be placed upon this green.

The charm of these single-streeted villages is too real to be lost, but they are gradually passing away before the rising tide of population and improvement. The

chief destructive agent is the trolley and in some places there is fierce opposition to the introduction of electric-cars by those who love the old state of things. Apropos of the protest that the summer residents of Deerfield, Massachusetts, are, at this writing, making against the coming of an electric-car line, the *Springfield Republican* says: "The opposition in the old street is not to the road, but to its great and inevitable detriment to the street. That old village is a great historic monument, and it owes its preservation chiefly to the people who have come into it in recent years because of its associations, historical and often ancestral, or because of its fine quiet and Old World air of rest. A singular endeavor has been shown to depreciate these people as 'summer visitors.' But not of one these households which have made their home on the street has anything like wealth—more, there is not one whose members are not engaged in work for their living. Some of these find their work in various cities, and live in them in the season of work; some remain in Deerfield all the year round, but work all the time. This is the meanest attack on public-spirited residents and taxpayers of the town, who love the old street and want to preserve it not only for themselves, but for the state and the nation, as an object-lesson of history." Possibly the protestants will win, more probably it will be the railway, and fine trees will lose their limbs, wires and their supporting parts will bring the old street nearer to the fashions of the day, and, in large measure, the pristine charm of quiet and quaintness, which those who know it relish so keenly, will have passed away forever. — WARE

THE "NOON HOUSE"

We do not know where in New England there still stands in its original form that precursor of the parish-parlor of today, the "Noon House." The early meeting houses were ill-heated in winter or not heated at all, and though the worshippers, doubtless, provided themselves with heated stones and foot-stoves, these primitive heaters could not last through even a protracted morning session, much less that of the afternoon, also. Therefore as a mere matter of self-preservation there was built near the meeting house a smaller structure, called the "Noon House," furnished with an ample fireplace. Here the congregation assembled, between morning and afternoon services, thawed out their chilled bodies, replenished their foot-stoves and reheated the more primitive stone or brick, ate their midday lunches and, while the elders presumably gossiped in a seemly and subdued way, the youths and maidens as certainly took the opportunity to flirt with due discreetness. — WARE

Porch of the old First-Church.

The First Church built 1681.

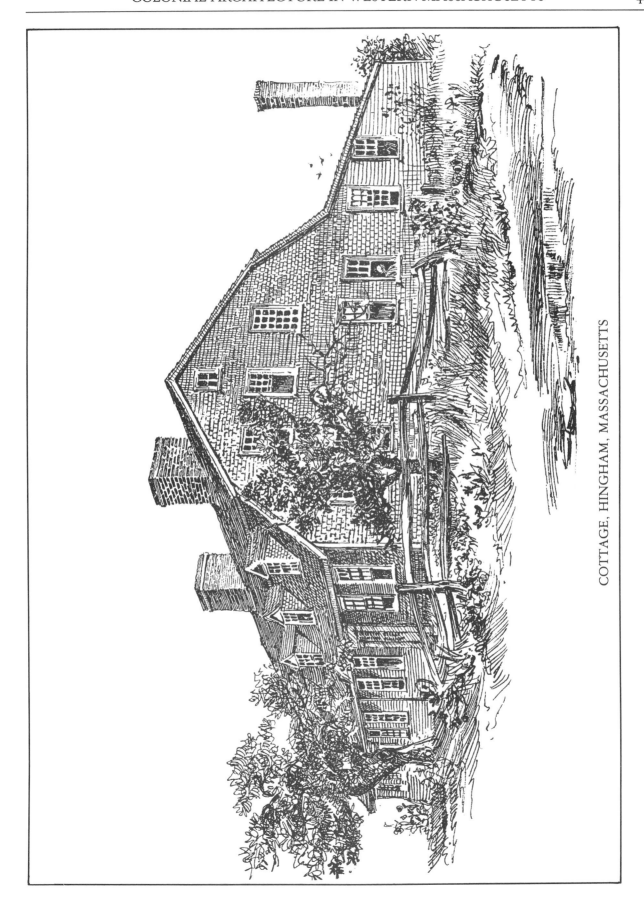

COTTAGE, HINGHAM, MASSACHUSETTS

COTTAGE, HINGHAM, MASSACHUSETTS

DUMMER HOUSE, BYFIELD, MASSACHUSETTS

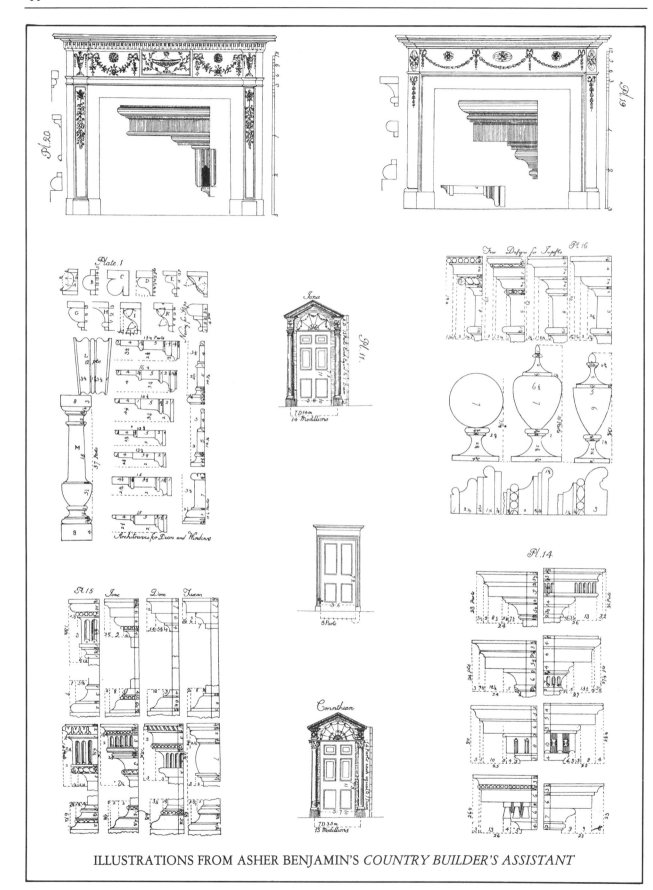

ILLUSTRATIONS FROM ASHER BENJAMIN'S *COUNTRY BUILDER'S ASSISTANT*

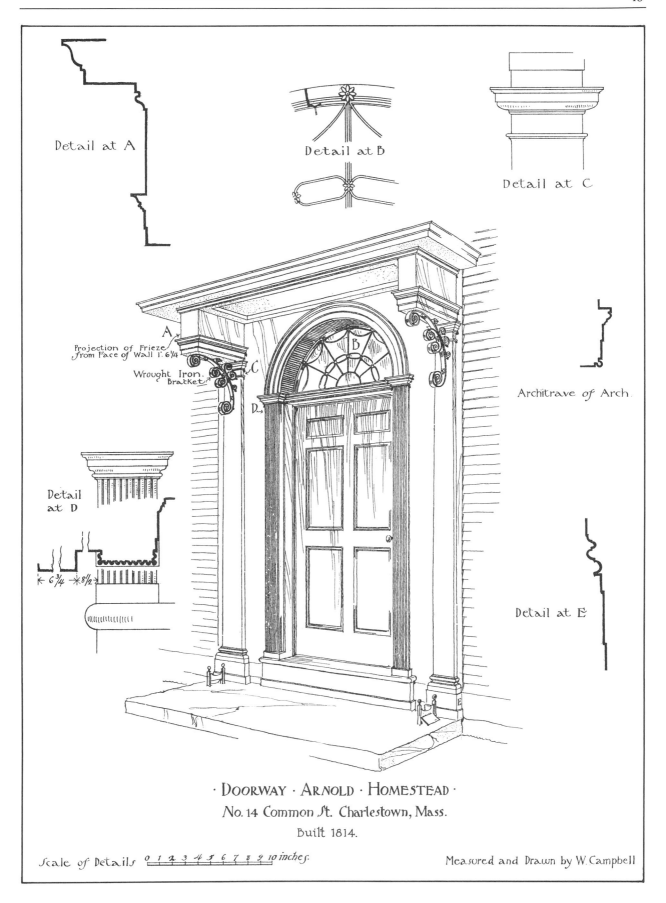

Detail at A

Detail at B

Detail at C

Projection of Frieze
from Face of Wall 1'. 6¼

Wrought Iron.
Bratket.

Architrave of Arch.

Detail
at D

6¾   8½

Detail at E

· DOORWAY · ARNOLD · HOMESTEAD ·

No. 14 Common St. Charlestown, Mass.

Built 1814.

Scale of Details   0 1 2 3 4 5 6 7 8 9 10 inches.

Measured and Drawn by W. Campbell

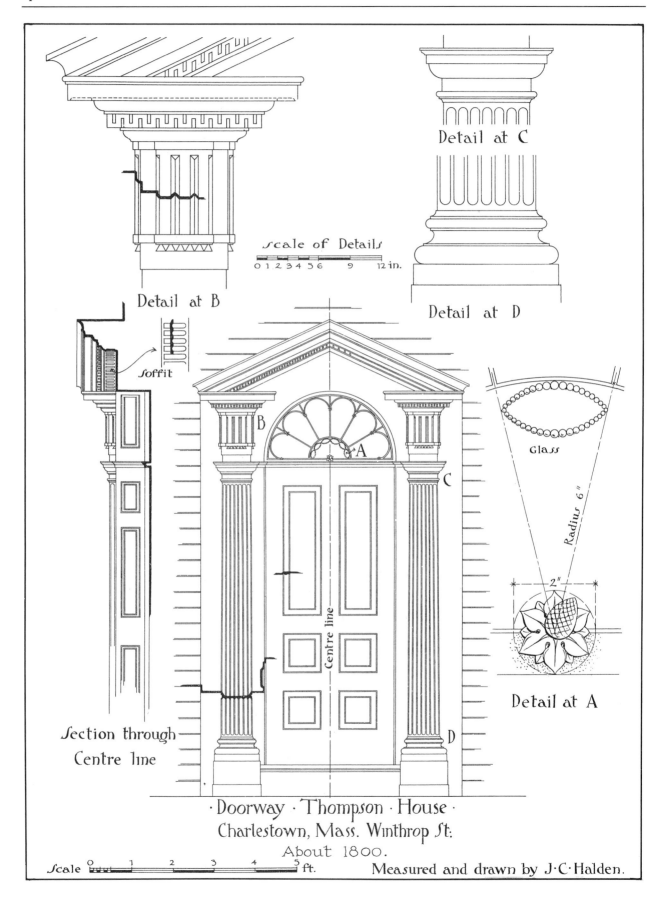

Detail at B

Detail at C

scale of Details
0 1 2 3 4 5 6   9   12 in.

Detail at D

soffit

B

A

C

Glass

Radius 6"

2"

Detail at A

D

Section through
Centre line

Centre line

· Doorway · Thompson · House ·
Charlestown, Mass. Winthrop St.
About 1800.

Scale 0 1 2 3 4 5 ft.   Measured and drawn by J·C·Halden.

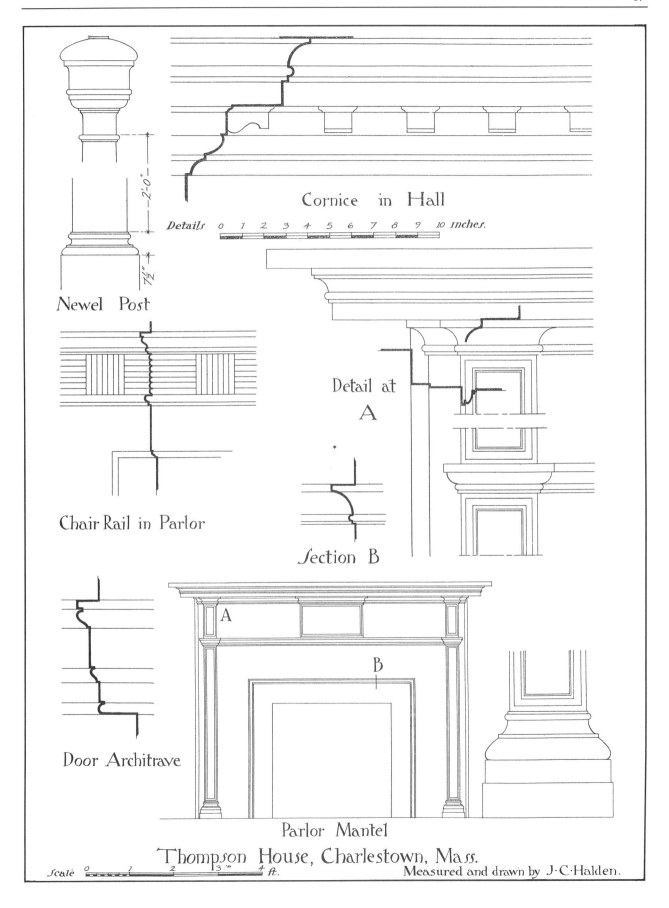

Cornice in Hall

Details 0 1 2 3 4 5 6 7 8 9 10 *inches.*

Newel Post

Chair Rail in Parlor

Detail at
A

Section B

Door Architrave

A

B

Parlor Mantel

Thompson House, Charlestown, Mass.

Scale 0 1 2 3 4 ft.

Measured and drawn by J·C·Halden.

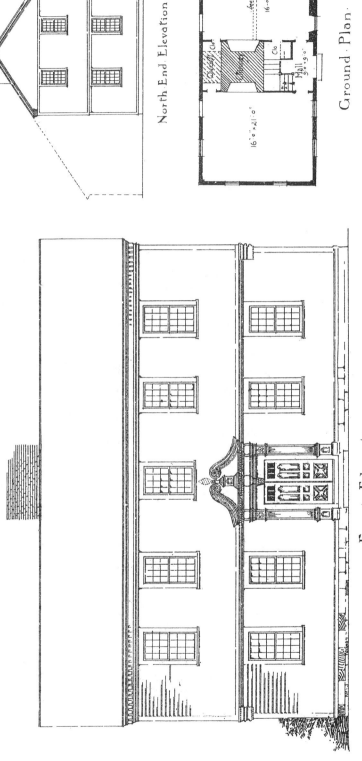

· HOUSE · AT · HADLEY · MASS ·
· BUILT · IN · 1713 ·

· · MEASURED · & · DRAWN · BY · G·C·GARDNER ·

Front Elevation

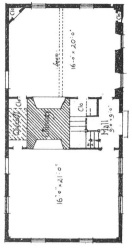

North End Elevation

Ground · Plan

Sketch by G·C·Gardner.

Dwight House 1769

JOSIAH · DWIGHT · HOUSE · 1764 · SPRINGFIELD · MASS ·

·M·I·T· Summer·School· 1895·

·Drawn·by·Ambrose·Walker·

HOUSES · IN ·

·DANVERSPORT·

·Massachusetts·

·Base Board·

·Cornice· of· Room·

·Architrave·

·Wainscot· of· Caps·

0   1   2   3 ft
·Scale· of· Mantels·

0 1 2 3 4 5 6 ins
·Scale· of· Details·

·Measured· by· Julius· F· Gaylor & Ambrose·Walker·

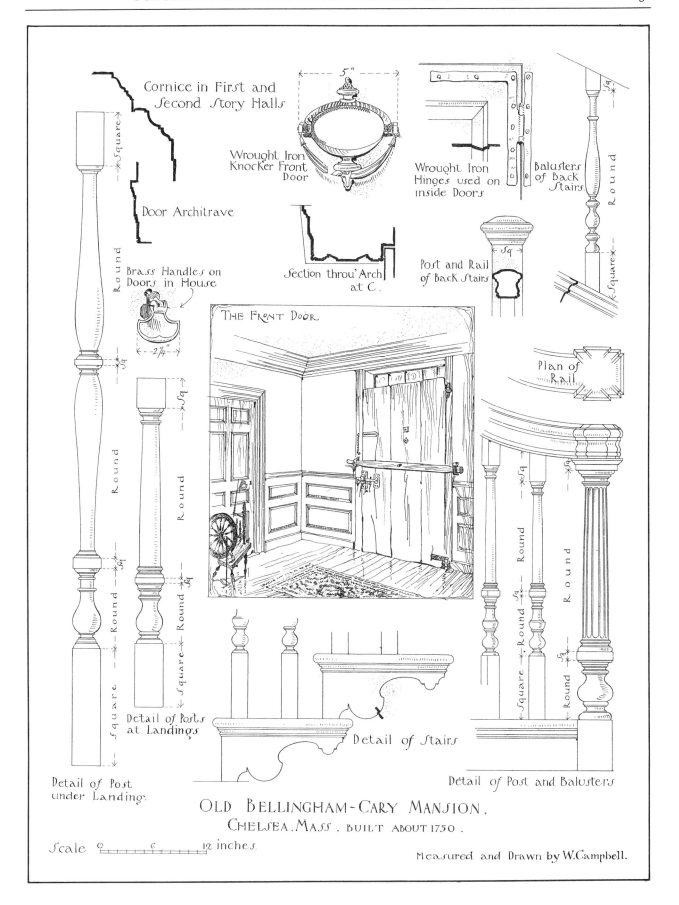

Cornice in First and Second Story Halls

Door Architrave

Round

Square

Brass Handles on Doors in House

2 1/4"

Round

Round

Square

Detail of Posts at Landings

Detail of Post under Landing.

Wrought Iron Knocker Front Door

5"

Section throu' Arch at C.

THE FRONT DOOR

Detail of Stairs

Wrought Iron Hinges used on inside Doors

Post and Rail of Back Stairs

Balusters of Back Stairs

Round

Square

Plan of Rail

Round

Square

Round

Square

Round

Detail of Post and Balusters

OLD BELLINGHAM-CARY MANSION, CHELSEA, MASS, BUILT ABOUT 1750.

Scale 0 6 12 inches

Measured and Drawn by W. Campbell.

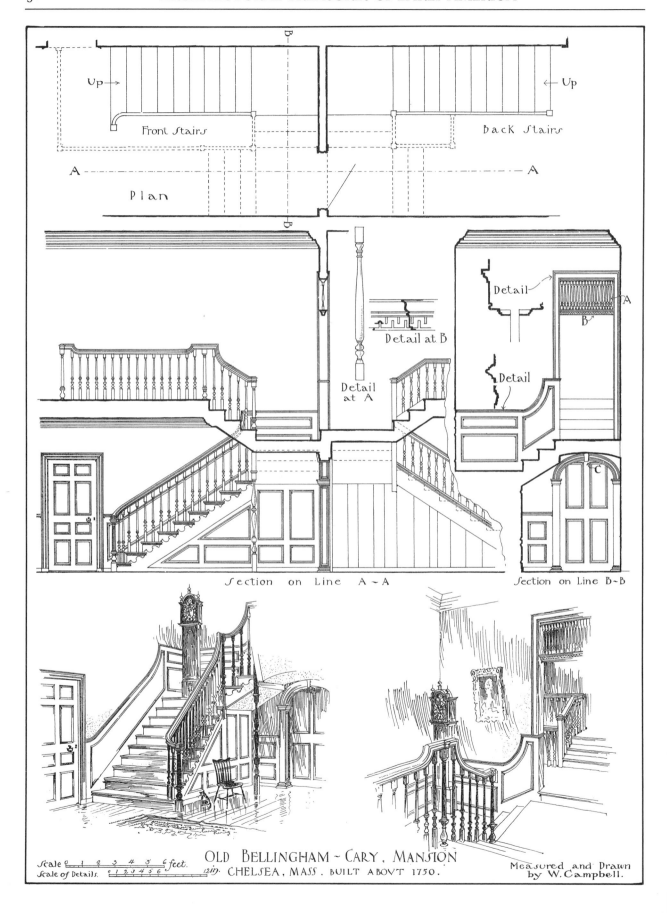

Up →   ← Up

Front Stairs   Back Stairs

A —————————————————————— A

Plan

Detail at B

Detail at A

Detail

Detail

Section on Line A ~ A

Section on Line B~B

Scale 0 1 2 3 4 5 6 feet.
Scale of Details. 0 1 2 3 4 5 6
12 in.

OLD BELLINGHAM ~ CARY, MANSION
CHELSEA, MASS. BUILT ABOVT 1750.

Measured and Drawn
by W. Campbell.

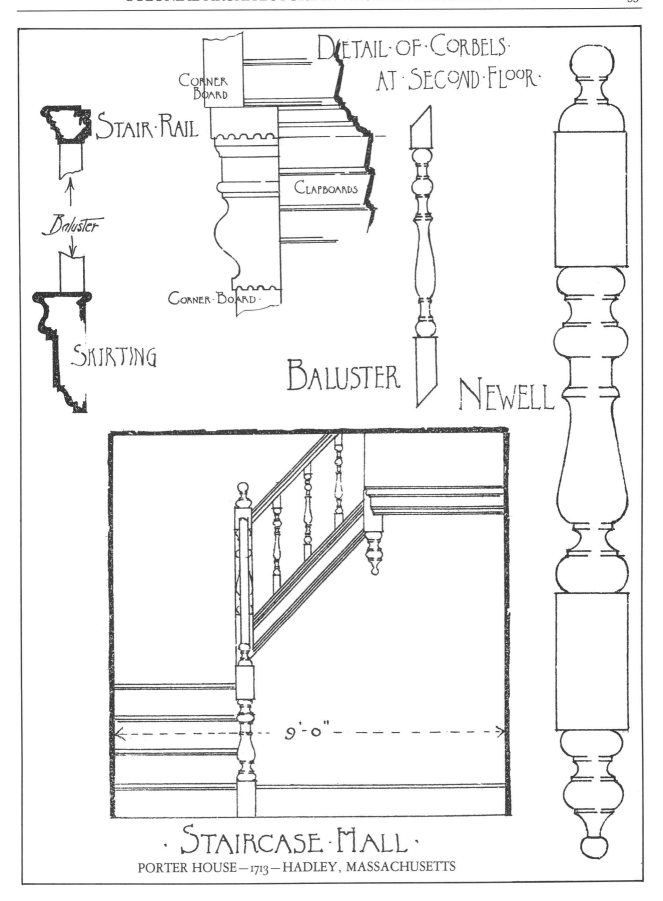

STAIR·RAIL

Baluster

SKIRTING

CORNER BOARD

DETAIL·OF·CORBELS·
AT·SECOND·FLOOR·

CLAPBOARDS

CORNER·BOARD·

BALUSTER

NEWELL

9'-0"

·STAIRCASE·HALL·

PORTER HOUSE — 1713 — HADLEY, MASSACHUSETTS

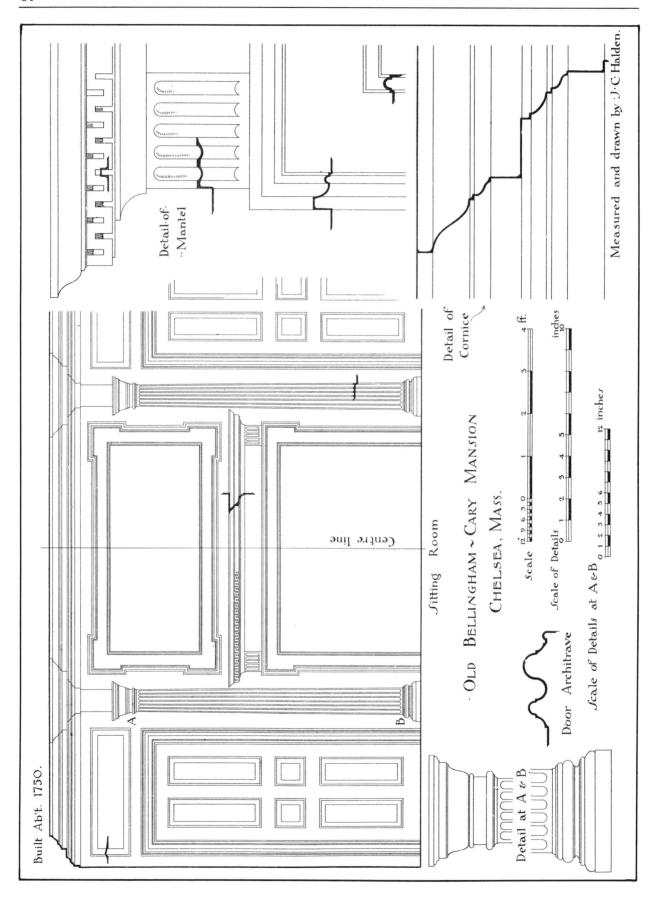

Built Ab't. 1750.

Detail of Mantel

Detail of Cornice

Sitting Room

Centre line

OLD BELLINGHAM ~ CARY MANSION
CHELSEA, MASS.

Scale

Scale of Details

Scale of Details at A & B

12 inches

Door Architrave

Detail at A & B

Measured and drawn by J·C·Halden.

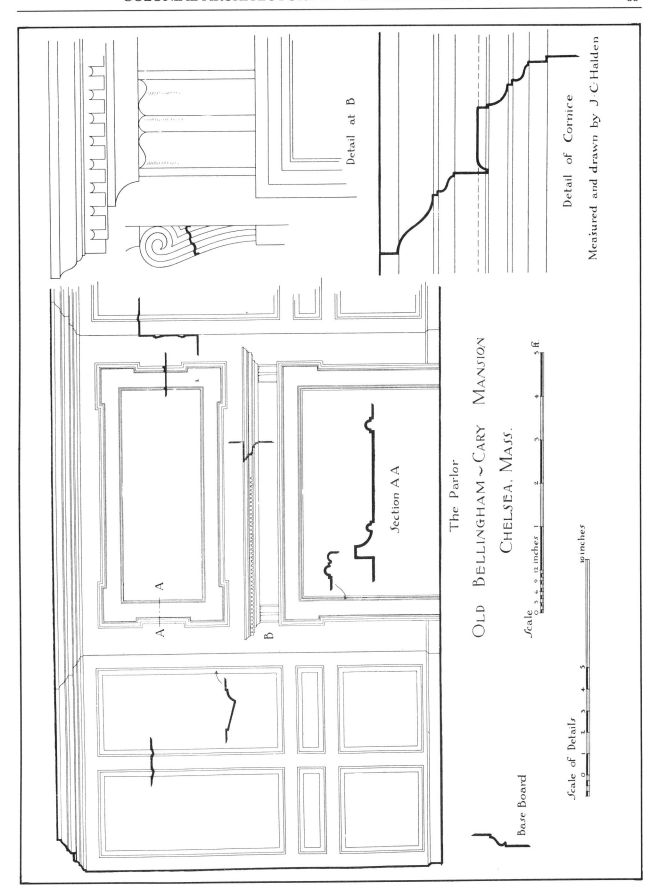

Detail at B

Detail of Cornice

Measured and drawn by J·C·Halden

Section A A

The Parlor

OLD BELLINGHAM ~ CARY MANSION

CHELSEA, MASS.

Scale
0 3 6 9 12 inches 1

10 inches

Scale of Details
0 1 2 3 4 5

Base Board

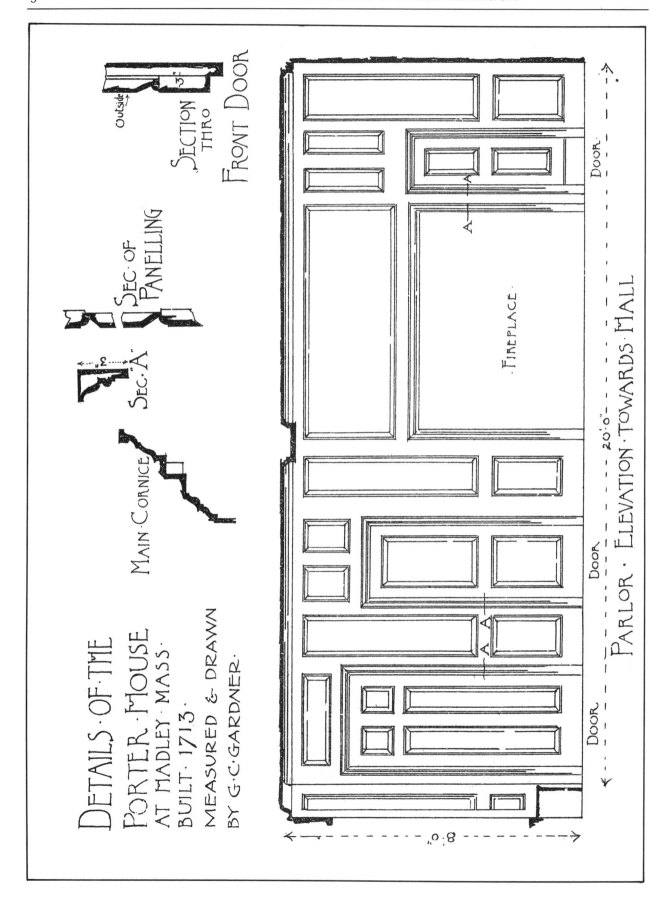

SECTION THRO FRONT DOOR

Outside

SEC OF PANELLING

SEC "A"

MAIN CORNICE

DETAILS OF THE
PORTER HOUSE
AT HADLEY MASS
BUILT 1713
MEASURED & DRAWN
BY G C GARDNER

FIREPLACE

DOOR

DOOR

DOOR

PARLOR ELEVATION TOWARDS HALL

Six Hours in
Salem, Massachusetts

Text by
Claude Fayette Bragdon
Originally published in 1899 as
Volume I of The Georgian Period

FAIRBANKS HOUSE — 1636 — DEDHAM, MASSACHUSETTS

SIX HOURS IN SALEM, MASSACHUSETTS

THE materials for the accompanying drawings and sketches, and the following facts, relative and irrelevant thereto, were collected by the present writer and a friend in a six-hour-long visit to Salem, supplemented by a short preliminary cramming at the Boston Library on the evening previous thereto. In so short a time, and with imperfect facilities (our only instruments were notebooks, rules and pencils, and a Kodak camera), it is perhaps presumptuous to suppose that much of fresh interest or of permanent value could be gathered in a field already so well harvested by such men as Arthur Little, Frank Wallis and others not less competent, but it so happened, partly by accident and partly also from design, that we devoted our attention principally to houses not treated before. In so doing we have hoped not only to escape comparisons, sure to be disastrous, but also to augment, in some slight degree, the sum total of drawings and documents pertaining to Colonial architecture in America.

In the popular mind, Salem is so indissolubly associated with the idea of witchcraft that in any article on the subject, however practical its nature or prosaic its style, it would be impossible not to refer in passing to that insane delusion, the horrid and bloody results of which have made the town famous not in the history of the country merely but in that of humanity at large. Indeed, the tragedy enacted there two centuries ago colors the life of the place today, and, like a murderer's conscience, clamors for recognition. There is a sinister something in the names one hears, such as the "Witch House" and "Gallows Hill"; the very word "witch," which once struck terror to brave hearts, is used now by tradesmen to enhance the value of their wares. In the court house are still to be seen the documents relating to the trials, and objects used as evidence; among them the "witch-pins" with which the accused were supposed to have tormented their victims. On the corner of Washington and Lynde streets we came upon a black bronze tablet bearing the following inscription:—

"Nearly opposite this spot stood, in the middle of the street, a building devoted from 1677 until 1718 to municipal and judicial uses. In it, in 1692, were tried and condemned for witchcraft most of the nineteen persons who suffered death on the gallows. Giles Corey was here put to trial on the same charge, and, refusing to plead, was taken away and pressed to death. In January, 1693, twenty-one persons were tried here for witchcraft, of whom eighteen were acquitted and three condemned, but later set free, together with about 150 accused persons in a general delivery which occurred in May."

It was like encountering a funeral on the street, and, hurried and preoccupied as we were, we could not but pause, and try to realize, if only for an instant, the terror which ruled the community when husbands accused wives, and children parents, and safety lay neither in wealth nor station—least of all in innocence—and fear and cowardice passed like a pestilence from heart to heart.

In reading over the reports of the witch trials one is afflicted by a feeling of something uncanny in it all, and is tempted to believe in witchcraft—obsession by evil spirits, and the rest; but time has strangely reversed the positions of accuser and accused, for now it is the judges who appear to be the vehicle of the diabolic will, so blind and implacable they seem—so in-

ON GALLOWS HILL

tent on having the blood of their victims. A single instance will suffice to illustrate this: One of the afflicted girls declared that Sarah Good, then on trial, had cut her with a knife and broken the blade in her flesh. Search was made, and, sure enough, the blade was found on Sarah's person. A young man, thereupon, arose and exposed the fraud. He produced the remainder of the knife, and told how he had thrown the broken blade away in the presence of the girl; but the court, instead of admitting his evidence, dismissed him with an admonition not to tell lies and continued the taking of testimony. What wonder that justice such as this wrung from Martha Corey the pathetic protest: "You are all against me and I cannot help it!"

Next to its having been the center of the witchcraft delusion, Salem is perhaps most famous as the birthplace of Nathaniel Hawthorne and the supposed scene of many of his romances. The house where he was born, and others in which he lived at various times, may still be seen by the curious visitor, and so intermingled do the real and the ideal become with the lapse of time that one of the principal "objects of interest" is a house supposed to have been the original of the "Seven Gables," though there is little or no evidence in support of such an assumption. Whatever may have once been its condition, it certainly tallies ill with Hawthorne's description; and of gables we counted only two. The Pickering House came much nearer our own ideal — even to the magnificent old elm before the door. These two are about the only remaining examples of the many and steep-gabled houses built here in the middle of the seventeenth century, in evident imitation of the Gothic half-timbered cottages of England.

We visited the Customhouse, where Hawthorne served a term in the capacity of Surveyor of the Port, an experience which he subsequently immortalized in his introduction to the *Scarlet Letter*. The place looks today exactly as he there describes it: —

"In my native town of Salem, at the head of what, half a century ago, in the days of old King Darby, was a bustling wharf, — but which is now burdened with decayed wooden warehouses, and exhibits few or no symptoms of commercial life; except, perhaps, a bark or brig, half way down its melancholy length, discharging hides; or, nearer at hand, a Nova Scotia schooner pitching out her cargo of firewood, — at the head, I say, of this dilapidated wharf, which the tide often overflows, and along which, at the base and in the rear of the row of buildings, the track of many languid years is seen in a border of unthrifty grass, — here, with a view from its front windows adown this not very enlivening prospect, and thence across the harbor, stands a spacious edifice of brick. From the loftiest point of its roof, during precisely three-and-a-half hours of each forenoon, floats or droops, in breeze or calm, the banner of the Republic; but with the thirteen stripes turned vertically, instead of horizontally, and thus indicating that a civil, and not a military, post of Uncle Sam's Government is here established. Its front is ornamented with a portico of half a dozen wooden pillars supporting a balcony, beneath which a flight of wide granite steps descends towards the street. Over the entrance hovers an enormous specimen of the American eagle, with outspread wings, a shield before her breast, and, if I recollect aright, a bunch of intermingled thunderbolts and barbed arrows in each claw."

Fresh from a reperusal of Hawthorne's description of his life there, we tried to imagine him as still an incumbent of the post, going about his accustomed duties, and we almost duped ourselves into believing that we would see his familiar figure within each newly opened door. There was little to discourage such a fancy. For aught that we could see, he might have left there only yesterday. The same superannuated sea-captains, apparently, slouched about the corridors, calling one another "Cap," and discussing the last or coming "clam fry," just as they did when Hawthorne passed among them like a prince disguised among his poor — he alone conscious of his rank and power, and waiting till the time came to declare it. One of the above-mentioned dignitaries showed us the window at which Hawthorne worked, and the chamber in which

PICKERING HOUSE

he found the scarlet letter (if he ever found it, except in a chamber of his brain), in a manner which showed it to be an accustomed service.

The building itself, erected about the beginning of the century, impressed us as a fine example of later Colonial architecture, full of dignity and repose, and, though scarcely larger than some of the houses with which it is surrounded, expressing in unmistakable and appropriate terms its character and office.

Hawthorne is by no means the only illustrious son of Salem. Prescott was born here; here Roger Williams taught and preached, and Count Rumford kept a store. Washington and Lafayette both visited the little town in the stirring Revolutionary days, and almost all of the presidents since. It is said that the first armed resistance to British authority occurred at the North Bridge in an engagement known as "Leslie's Retreat." In the war of 1812 the battle between the *Chesapeake* and the *Shannon* was fought off the shore of Salem, and was witnessed from the hills by the townspeople.

But more interesting to us than the town's history were the lovely old houses of which it is built up.

We had come to see them and to this purpose we devoted our remaining time. To the mind of an architect the buildings of Salem arrange themselves naturally into three classes: First, those very old houses, built by early settlers in the most primitive times, possessing all the dignity and simplicity and, withal, the barrenness of the Puritan character, and around which cluster many strange, true histories and curious traditions; second, those built in later Colonial and Revolutionary days, usually by rich merchants and ship-owners, when Salem had become a principal port of entry, and an important commercial center, and in which the Colonial style is exhibited in its very flower; and third, those purely modern structures—confused, chaotic— which have sprung up in profusion in some parts of the town, like weeds in an old-fashioned garden.

The very oldest house of all, as well as the most famous, is the Roger Williams House, on the corner of Essex and North streets. The exact date of its building is not known, but it cannot be far short of three centuries ago, for in 1675 the chimneys had to be taken down and rebuilt. It again suffered alteration in 1746,

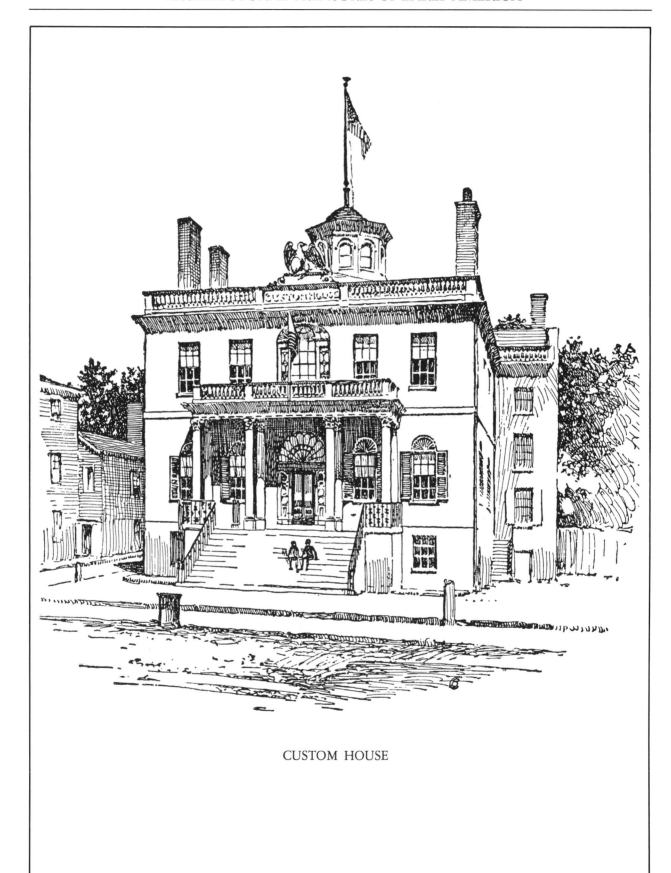

CUSTOM HOUSE

A SALEM BACK YARD

PINGREE HOUSE

and now a vulgar little modern drugstore grows out of its withered old side, like some excrescence, indicative of age and disease and swift-coming disolution. The western portion, with its quaint, overhanging second story, is almost all that remains of the original structure, but from it, in imagination, one may reconstruct the whole.

In 1635 this house was the home of Roger Williams, and from it he was driven by Puritanical intolerance to seek shelter among the Indians at Narragansett Bay, where he founded the state of Rhode Island, as every schoolboy knows. In a letter to his friend, Major Williams, he thus refers to the event which drove him thither:

"When I was unkindly and unchristianly, as I believe, driven from my house and land and wife and children (in the midst of a New England winter, now about thirty-five years past) at Salem, that ever honored Governor, Mr. Winthrop, privately wrote to me to steer my course to the Nahigonset Bay and Indians for many high and heavenly and publike ends encouraging me from the freenes of the place from any English claims or patents. I took his prudent motion as an hint and voice from God, and waving all other thoughts and motives I steered my course from Salem (through winter snows which I feel yet) into these parts where I may say Peniel, that is, I have seene the face of God."

The house passed then into the possession of Captain Richard Davenport, whose administrators sold it in 1675 to Jonathan Corwin, notorious as being one of the two magistrates before whom were tried and condemned those first persons, "charged with certain detestable arts called witchcraft and sorceries wickedly and feloniously used, practiced and exercised by which the persons named were tortured, afflicted, pineol, consumed, wasted and tormented." The preliminary examinations of some of the accused are said to have taken place in a room of the old house, and this circumstance has given it the name of the "Witch House," by which it is best known.

In rummaging over some old files of the *Essex Institute Bulletin* in the Boston Library I came upon a transcript of the contract between Corwin and one Daniel Andrewe for remodeling the house. I give it here entire. As an example of an early specification, it will be seen to possess all the diffuseness and obscurity common to such documents at the present time:

"The said Daniel Andrewe is to dig and build a cellar as large as the easterly room of said house will afford (and in the said room according to the breadthe and length of it) not exceeding six foot in height; and to underpin the porch and the remaining part of the house not exceeding one foot; the said kitchen being 20 feet long and 18 feet wide; and to make steps with stones into the cellar in two places belonging to the cellar, together with stone steps up into the porch. 2. For the chimney he is to take down the chimneys which are now standing, and to take and make up of the bricks that are now in the chimneys, and the stones that are in the lean-to cellar that now is, and to rebuild the said chimney with five fireplaces viz: two below and two in the chambers and one in the garret; also to build one chimney in the kitchen with ovens and a furnace, not exceeding five feet above the top of the house. 3. He is to set the jambs of the two chamber chimneys and of the easternmost room below with Dutch tiles, the said owner finding the tiles; also to lay all the hearths belonging to the said house and to point the cellar and underpinning of sd. house and so much of the hearths as are to be laid with Dutch tiles the said owner is to find them. 4. As for lathing and plaistering he is to lath and siele the four rooms of the house betwixt the joists overhead and to plaister the sides of the house with a coat of lime and haire upon the clay; also to fill the gable ends of the house with bricks and to plaister them with clay. 5. To lath and plaister the partitions of the house with clay and lime and to fill, lath and plaister the porch and porch chambers and to plaister them with lime and haire besides; and to siele and lath them overhead with lime and to fill, lath and plaister the kitchen up to the wall plate on every side. The said Daniel Andrewe is to find lime, bricks, clay, stone, haire together with labourers and workmen to help him, and generally all the materials for effecting and carrying out of the aforesaid worke, except laths and nails. 7. The whole work before mentioned is to be done finished and performed att or before the last day of August next following

provided the said Daniel or any that work with him be not lett or hindered for want of the carpenter worke. 8. Lastly, in consideration of the aforesaid worke, so finished and accomplished as aforesaid, the aforesaid owner is to pay or cause to be paid unto the said workmen the summe of fifty pounds in money current in New England, to be paid at or before the finishing of the said worke. And for the true performance of the premises, we bind ourselves each to other, our heyeres, executors and administrators, firmly by these presents, as witnesse our hands, this nineteenth day of February, Anno Domini 1674–5.

JONATHAN CORWIN
DANIEL ANDREWE"

The meeting house in which Roger Williams used to preach—the first for congregational worship built in America—has been carefully restored and preserved, and stands now in the rear of the Essex Institute. The frame is about all that remains of the original building.[1] It is so small that a person reaching forward from the front of the gallery might touch the extended hand of the minister behind the desk. It is used as a repository for many curious relics, among them Hawthorne's desk, at which the *Scarlet Letter* was written, or at least begun.

The Pickering House, before alluded to, is also of great antiquity, having been built in 1651 by John Pickering, and inhabited ever since by his direct lineal descendants. For this reason, perhaps, it betrays few evidences of the ravages of time. There are other houses in Salem, built about the same time, which, though interesting historically, present few attractions to the lovers of architectural beauty. It was for those built about the year 1800 that we reserved our admiration and our lead pencils—great square structures, usually of brick and stone, with wooden cornices and porches. One of them, typical of the whole class, especially arrested our attention by the beauty of its proportions and detail. Standing a little back from the street, and apart from its neighbors on either side, it displayed a façade plain almost to barrenness, but so well fenestrated and divided horizontally by broad bands of brickwork at each floor-level as to quite fill and satisfy the eye. This wall was finished with a well-proportioned cornice, and this, in turn, surmounted by a delicate balustrade. The only other bit of ornament consisted in one of those dainty and beautiful

---

[1] During the current year Mr. Eben Putnam has brought forward an elaborate argument, which seeks to show that this cherished relic is not the first meeting house erected in 1634 and that, even if it is the earliest church building in Salem, still earlier churches were erected—the Boston and Cambridge churches in 1632 and the Dorchester church in 1633.—WARE

TYPICAL SALEM FRAME HOUSE

semicircular porches before the entrance, of which we saw so many in Salem. Through the courtesy of its occupants, we obtained admission to this house, and made drawings of much of its interior woodwork, which was both rich and refined. It was while so engaged that we first learned that the house had been the scene of one of the most horrible murders in all the history of crime, known at the time of its committal as the "Salem Murder," and celebrated alike for its cold-blooded brutality, the high position of many of the individuals concerned, and the singular succession of fatalities which accompanied and followed it. The facts are, briefly, these:

In a room of the old house, on the night of the 6th of April, 1830, Capt. Joseph White, a rich and respected citizen of Salem, was stabbed and beaten to death, as was alleged, by his nephews, George and Richard Crowninshield, and an accomplice, in order, it is supposed, to obtain possession of the old man's will. When the crime was discovered, the whole countryside was aroused, a great public meeting held, and the murderers hunted down and apprehended. In the trials which followed, some of the greatest lawyers in the country participated, among them Daniel Webster and Samuel Hoar. The jury failed to agree, and so the trials came to nothing; but they were full of startling and dramatic incidents. Chief Justice Isaac Parker, immediately after delivering his charge to the jury, fell forward, dead, and one of the Crowninshields killed himself in jail while waiting trial. The other, Richard, was the inventor of some of the most intricate machinery used in the factories of New England today.

This tale, when we heard it, somehow dampened our architectural ardors. At this window, we reflected, where now the sun streamed so bright in, the assassin entered; these floors creaked warningly beneath his stealthy feet, and then were treacherously still; this spotless white woodwork had been crimsoned by the old man's blood; these walls resounded with his dying groans. We did not care to linger after that, but tiptoed down the broad stairs and through the still hall out into the welcome noise and glare of Essex Street.

The Essex Institute was just next door, and we spent half an hour very pleasantly in the museum, where there are many pieces of fine old furniture and wood-

work taken from houses now destroyed. We found fine furniture, also, in the house of Major George Whipple, and the first "Salem cupboard" that we had ever seen.

A little beyond the Essex Institute is the armory of the Salem Cadets, a stately old house built by Col. Francis Peabody in 1818. Its front is diversified by two segment-shaped bays, in this respect a departure from the usual Salem type, though a common feature of many old houses in Boston. The interior is more than ordinarily grand, one room containing a white marble mantel with carved caryatides. Off of the stair-landing is a banqueting-hall finished in oak in Elizabethan Gothic, where, we are told by the guidebook, "Prince Arthur of England was entertained at dinner on the occasion of his attending the funeral of George Peabody, the banker, February 8, 1870." This rich, dark, elaborate interior is in startling contrast to the trim white Colonial finish of the rest of the house.

We left Salem for Boston about three in the afternoon, with such feelings of regret as must have been Sinbad's on quitting the Valley of Diamonds, for, to our unaccustomed Western eyes, the place seemed a veritable mine of architectural wealth. The permanent impression left with us by our hasty visit was of an exceedingly quaint and picturesque old town, striving here and there to be "smart" and modern, like some faded spinster who has seen better days, who mistakenly prefers our shoddy fabrics to the faded silks and yellow lace and other heirlooms of an opulent past. The old houses which we visited, as redolent with memories of other days as a rose that has been kissed and laid away, awoke in us a mood of pleasant melancholy full of vague guesses and conjectures. It was as though the houses themselves were trying to communicate to us their secrets, and had half succeeded. They seemed, indeed, human in a way that modern houses never do—like the Colonial dames, their mistresses—trim, plain and a bit prudish in outward appearance, but interiorly beautiful, full of fine and delicate sentiment. This comparison, fanciful perhaps, is yet applicable to the old houses of the South, which occupy their acres more invitingly, with less restraint, and are, altogether, more charming outwardly, yet, within, are not without a certain strain of coarseness.

NICHOLS HOUSE — 1801 — FEDERAL STREET, SALEM, MASSACHUSETTS

HODGES HOUSE — 1800 — ESSEX STREET, SALEM, MASSACHUSETTS

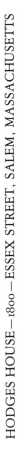

JOHN DERBY HOUSE, DERBY STREET, SALEM, MASSACHUSETTS

Photograph by Frank Cousins

JOSEPH CABOT HOUSE — 1810 — SALEM, MASSACHUSETTS

Photograph by Frank Cousins

EMERTON [FORMERLY PICKMAN] HOUSE — 1820 — ESSEX STREET,
SALEM, MASSACHUSETTS

Remodeled in 1885, by Arthur Little, Architect.

GEORGE PEABODY HOUSE — 1818 — SALEM, MASSACHUSETTS

SAFFORD [FORMERLY ANDREW] HOUSE — 1818 — SALEM, MASSACHUSETTS

CORNER OLIVER STREET AND WASHINGTON SQUARE, SALEM

20 TURNER STREET, SALEM

OSGOOD HOUSE, SALEM

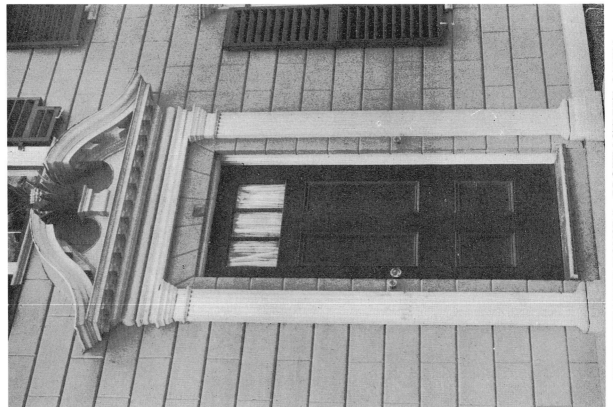

"THE PINEAPPLE HOUSE," 7 BROWN STREET, SALEM

LORD HOUSE, WASHINGTON STREET, SALEM

10 CHESTNUT STREET, SALEM

129 ESSEX STREET, SALEM

SAFFORD [ANDREW] HOUSE, WASHINGTON STREET, SALEM

GOVERNOR ENDICOTT'S HOUSE, 365 ESSEX STREET, SALEM

81 ESSEX STREET, SALEM, MASSACHUSETTS

NICHOLS HOUSE, FEDERAL STREET, SALEM

MRS. BOWDOIN'S HOUSE, SALEM

·M·I·T· Summer·School· 1895·

·After· drawings· by· M· J· Sturm·
·C· K· B· Nevin·

12 9 6 3 0 in. 1 ft.
·Scale ·for· Porch · & · Fence Post·

·OLIVER·HOUSE·
·142·Federal·St·
Salem, Mass.

·Front · Elevation ·
·Scale 0 5 10 15 20 25 30 ft.

0 1 2 3 6 12 in.
·Second · Story·Windows·

·Built · 1802·

·J·C·H·

WARD HOUSE, HERBERT STREET, SALEM, MASSACHUSETTS

STEARNS HOUSE, ESSEX STREET, SALEM, MASSACHUSETTS

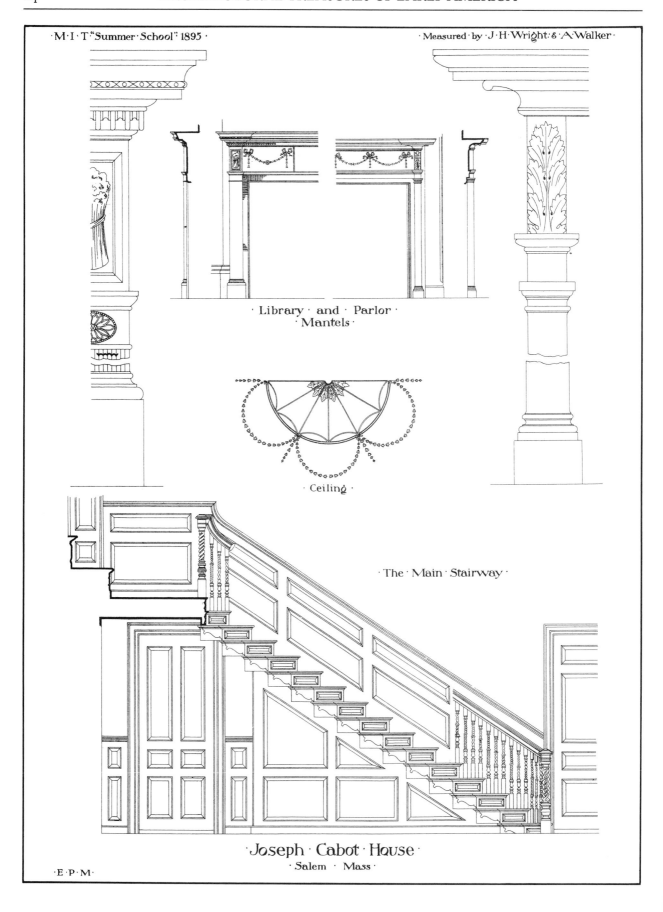

·M·I·T·"Summer·School"·1895·

·Measured·by·J·H·Wright·&·A·Walker·

· Library · and · Parlor ·
· Mantels ·

· Ceiling ·

· The · Main · Stairway ·

· Joseph · Cabot · House ·
· Salem · Mass ·

·E·P·M·

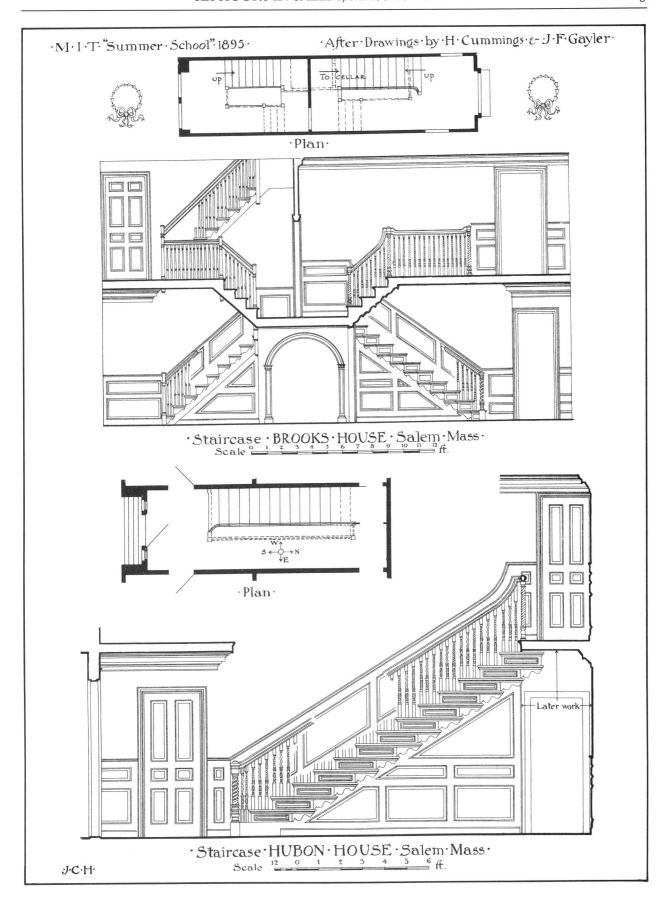

·M·I·T·"Summer·School"·1895·   ·After·Drawings·by·H·Cummings·&·J·F·Gayler·

·Plan·

·Staircase · BROOKS·HOUSE · Salem·Mass·
Scale 0 1 2 3 4 5 6 7 8 9 10 11 12 ft.

·Plan·

·Staircase·HUBON·HOUSE·Salem·Mass·
Scale 12 0 1 2 3 4 5 6 ft.

J·C·H·

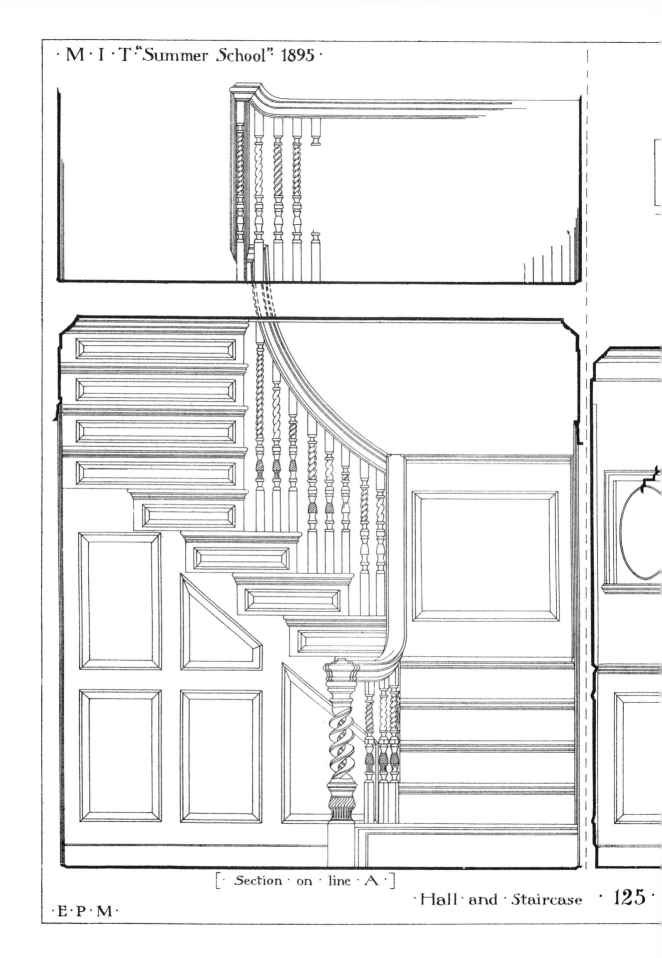

[· Section · on · line · A ·]

· Hall · and · Staircase · · 125 ·

·E·P·M·

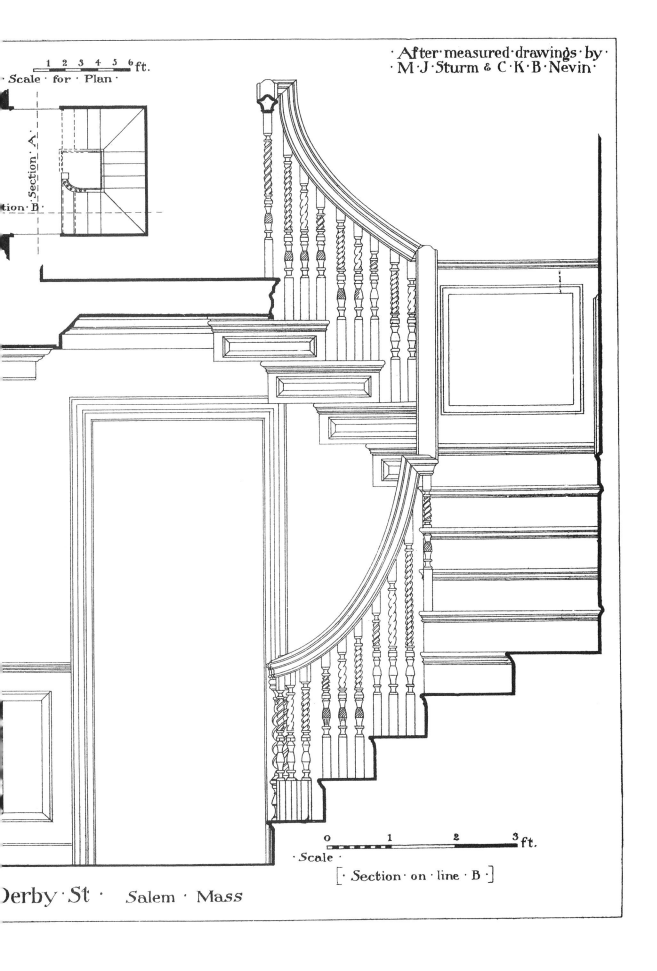

1 2 3 4 5 6 ft.
· Scale · for · Plan ·

· Section · A ·

tion · B ·

0 1 2 3 ft.
· Scale ·

[· Section · on · line · B ·]

Derby · St · Salem · Mass

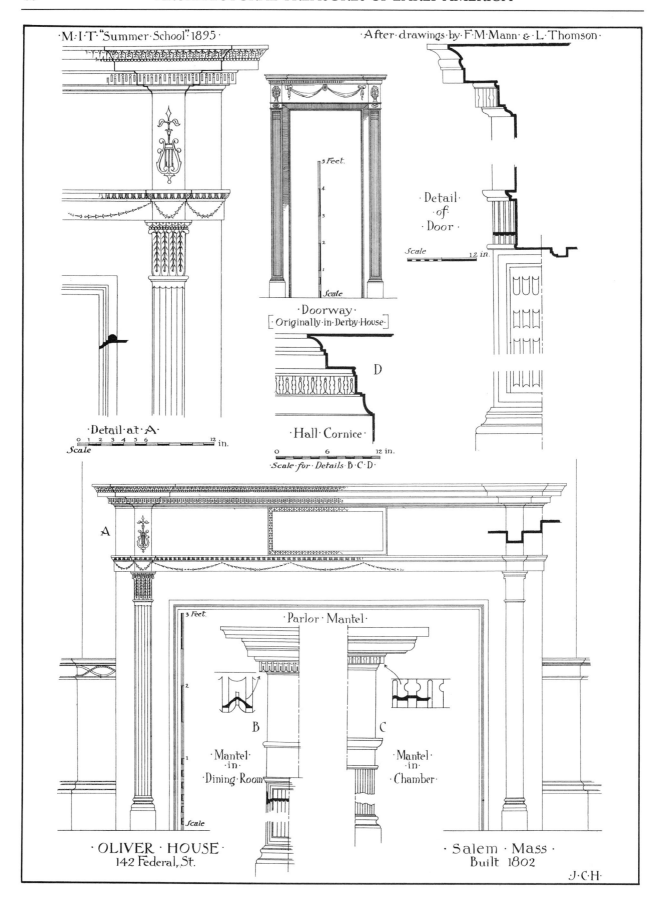

·M·I·T·"Summer·School"·1895·

·After·drawings·by·F·M·Mann·&·L·Thomson·

·Detail· ·of· ·Door·

Scale   12 in.

·Doorway·
[·Originally·in·Derby·House·]

D

·Hall·Cornice·

0   6   12 in.
·Scale·for·Details·B·C·D·

·Detail·at·A·
0 1 2 3 4 5 6   12 in.
Scale

3 Feet
4
3
2
1
Scale

A

·Parlor·Mantel·

3 Feet

2

B

·Mantel·
·in·
·Dining·Room·

C

·Mantel·
·in·
·Chamber·

1

Scale

·OLIVER·HOUSE·
142 Federal, St.

· Salem · Mass ·
Built 1802

·J·C·H·

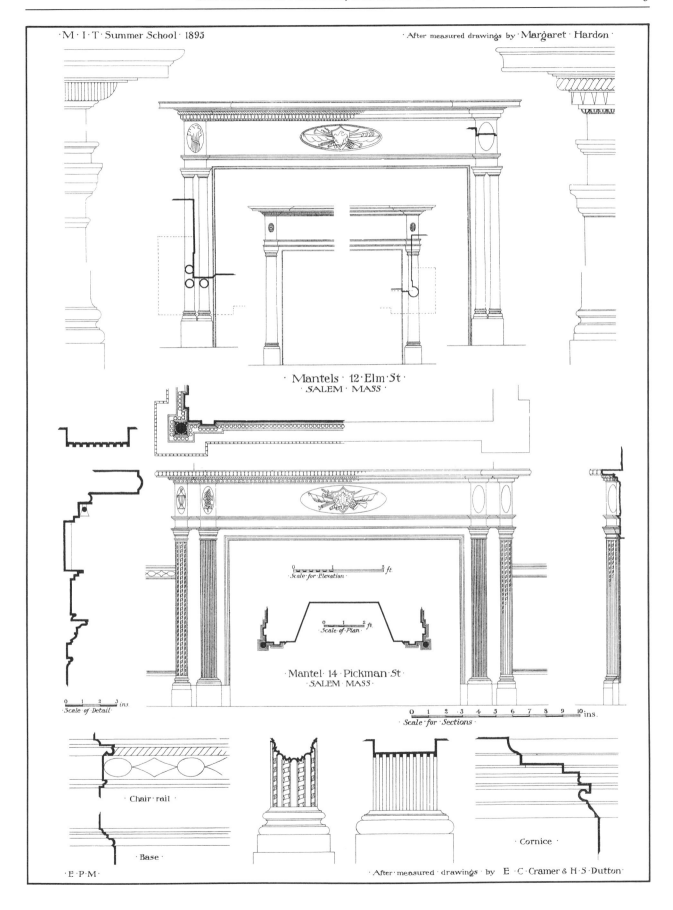

·M·I·T· Summer School· 1895

·After measured drawings by· Margaret · Hardon ·

· Mantels · 12·Elm·St ·
·SALEM· MASS·

·Scale·for·Elevation·
·Scale·of·Plan·

· Mantel· 14 ·Pickman·St ·
·SALEM· MASS·

·Scale·of·Detail·

· Scale · for · Sections ·

· Chair·rail ·

· Base ·

· Cornice ·

·E·P·M·

·After· measured · drawings · by· E ·C· Cramer & H ·S· Dutton ·

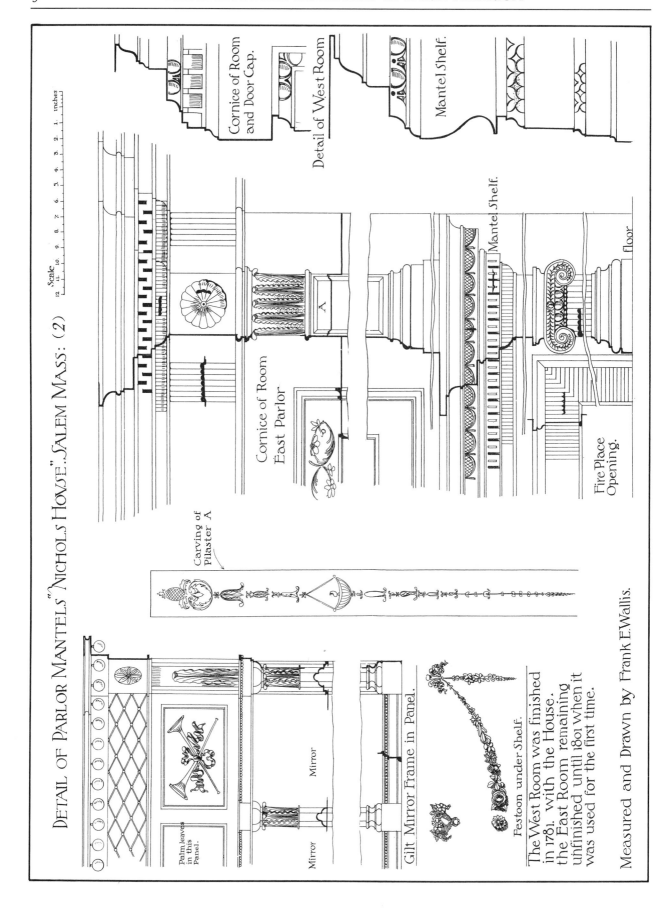

DETAIL OF PARLOR MANTELS "NICHOLS HOWSE", SALEM MASS: (2)

Scale
12. 11. 10. 9. 8. 7. 6. 5. 4. 3. 2. 1. inches

Cornice of Room and Door Cap.

Detail of West Room

Mantel Shelf.

Cornice of Room East Parlor

Mantel Shelf.

Fire Place Opening.

floor

Carving of Pilaster A

Palm leaves in this Panel.

Mirror

Mirror

Gilt Mirror Frame in Panel.

Festoon under Shelf.

The West Room was finished in 1781. with the House. the East Room remaining unfinished until 1801 when it was used for the first time.

Measured and Drawn by Frank E. Wallis.

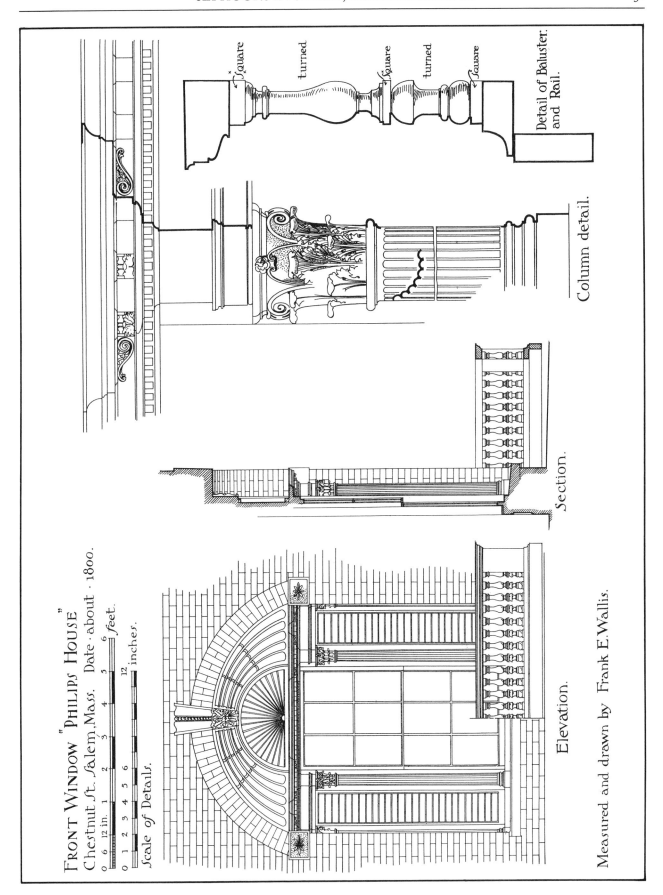

Detail of Baluster and Rail.

Square   turned   Square   turned   Square

Column detail.

Section.

Front Window "Philips House"
Chestnut St. Salem, Mass. Date · about · 1800.

feet.
inches.
Scale of Details.

Elevation.

Measured and drawn by Frank E. Wallis.

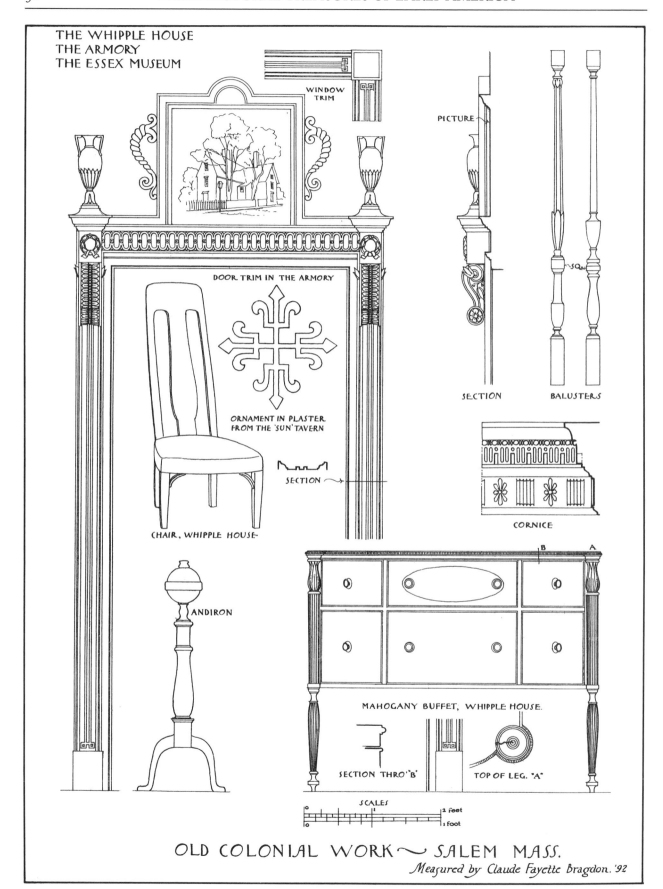

THE WHIPPLE HOUSE
THE ARMORY
THE ESSEX MUSEUM

WINDOW TRIM

PICTURE

DOOR TRIM IN THE ARMORY

ORNAMENT IN PLASTER
FROM THE 'SUN' TAVERN

SECTION

CHAIR, WHIPPLE HOUSE

SECTION   BALUSTERS

CORNICE

ANDIRON

MAHOGANY BUFFET, WHIPPLE HOUSE.

SECTION THRO' 'B'   TOP OF LEG. 'A'

SCALES   2 feet
                1 foot

OLD COLONIAL WORK ～ SALEM MASS.

Measured by Claude Fayette Bragdon. '92

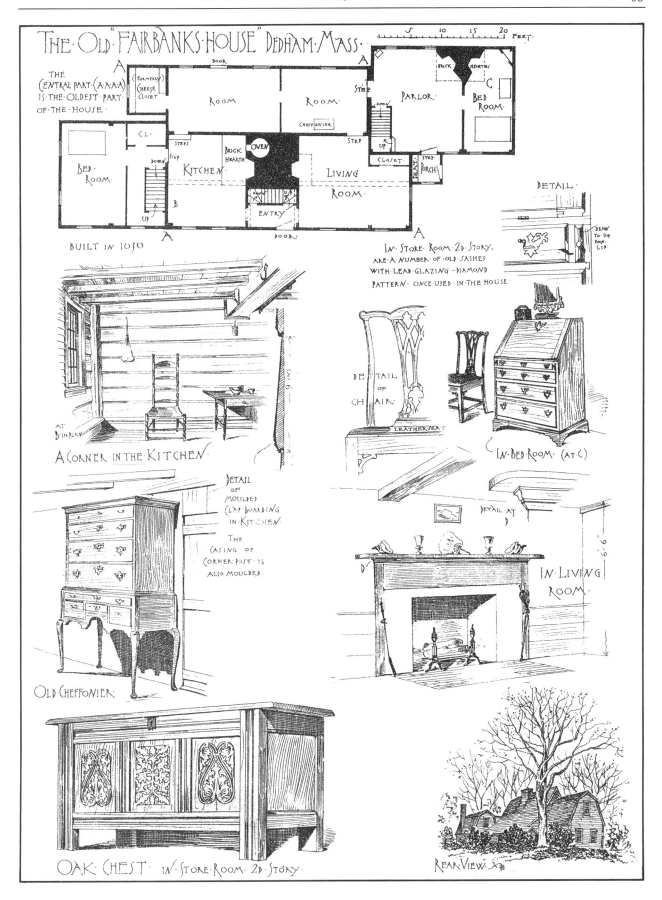

THE OLD "FAIRBANKS HOUSE" DEDHAM MASS.

5 10 15 20 FEET

THE CENTRAL PART (A A A A) IS THE OLDEST PART OF THE HOUSE

(FORMERLY CHEESE CLOSET)

DOOR

ROOM

ROOM

CHEFFONIER

BRICK HEARTH

STEP

PARLOR

BRICK HEARTH

BED ROOM C

CL

STEPS

STEP

BRICK HEARTH

OVEN

KITCHEN

STEP

DOWN

BED ROOM

DOWN

UP

CLOSET

STEP PORCH

SEAT

LIVING ROOM

B

UP

ENTRY

DOOR

A

BUILT IN 1636

IN STORE ROOM 2D STORY ARE A NUMBER OF OLD SASHES WITH LEAD GLAZING – DIAMOND PATTERN · ONCE USED IN THE HOUSE

DETAIL

DRAW TO SLIP BACK LID

A CORNER IN THE KITCHEN

AT B IN PLAN

9 INS

DETAIL OF CHAIR

LEATHER SEAT

IN BED ROOM (AT C)

DETAIL OF MOULDED CLAP BOARDING IN KITCHEN

THE CASING OF CORNER POST IS ALSO MOULDED

DETAIL AT D

D

IN LIVING ROOM

6 · 9

OLD CHEFFONIER

OAK CHEST · IN STORE ROOM 2D STORY

REAR VIEW

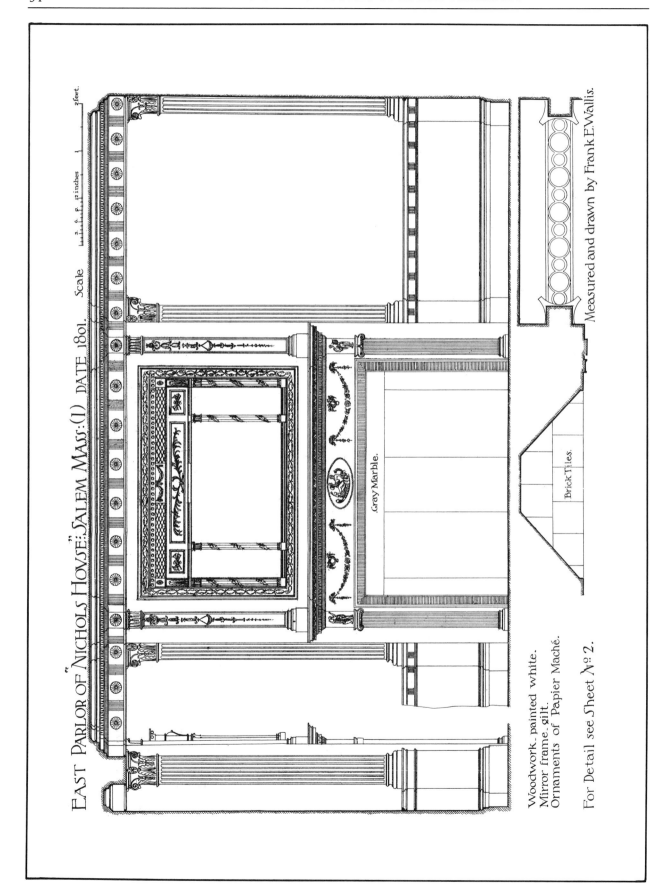

EAST PARLOR OF "NICHOLS HOWSE"::SALEM MASS:(1) DATE 1801.   Scale

Measured and drawn by Frank E. Wallis.

Gray Marble.

Brick Tiles.

Woodwork. painted white.
Mirror frame. gilt.
Ornaments of Papier Maché.

For Detail see Sheet No. 2.

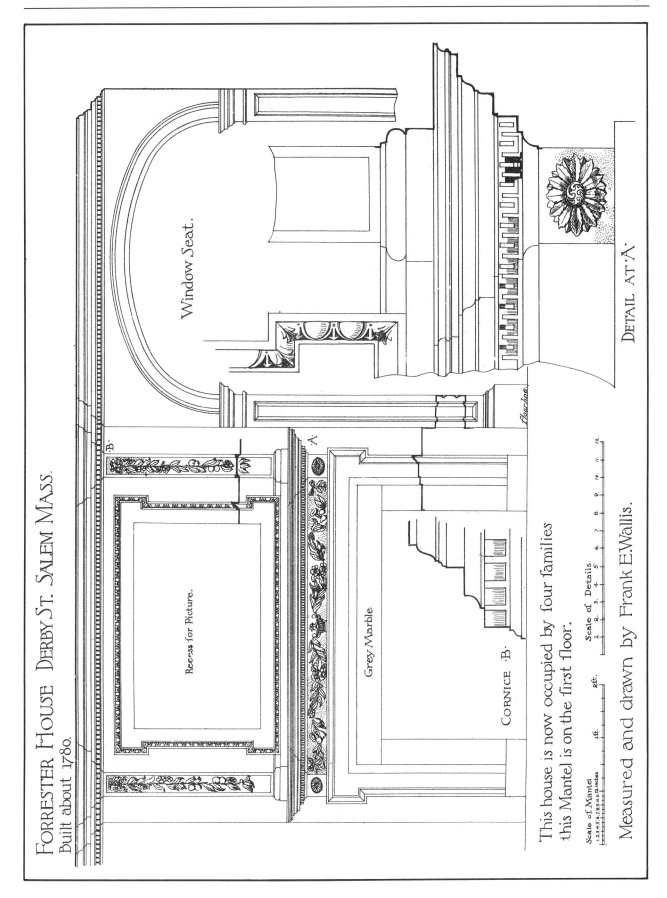

FORRESTER HOUSE DERBY ST. SALEM MASS.
Built about 1780.

Window Seat.

DETAIL AT ·A·

Recess for Picture.

·B·

·A·

Grey Marble

Floorline.

CORNICE ·B·

This house is now occupied by four families
this Mantel is on the first floor.

Scale of Mantel
2ft.   1ft.   2ft.
1.2.3.4.5.6.7.8.9.10.11.12.inches

Scale of Details.
1   2   3   4   5   6   7   8   9   10   11   12.

Measured and drawn by Frank E.Wallis.

MANTEL IN OFFICE OF "ESSEX HOVSE"
SALEM MASS. DATE 1801.
Measured and drawn by Frank E. Wallis.

DETAIL A.

DETAIL OF SHELF B.

DETAIL OF D.

DETAIL OF CENTERPIECE.

Scale

Scale of Details.

DETAIL OF PILASTER C.

DETAIL OF E

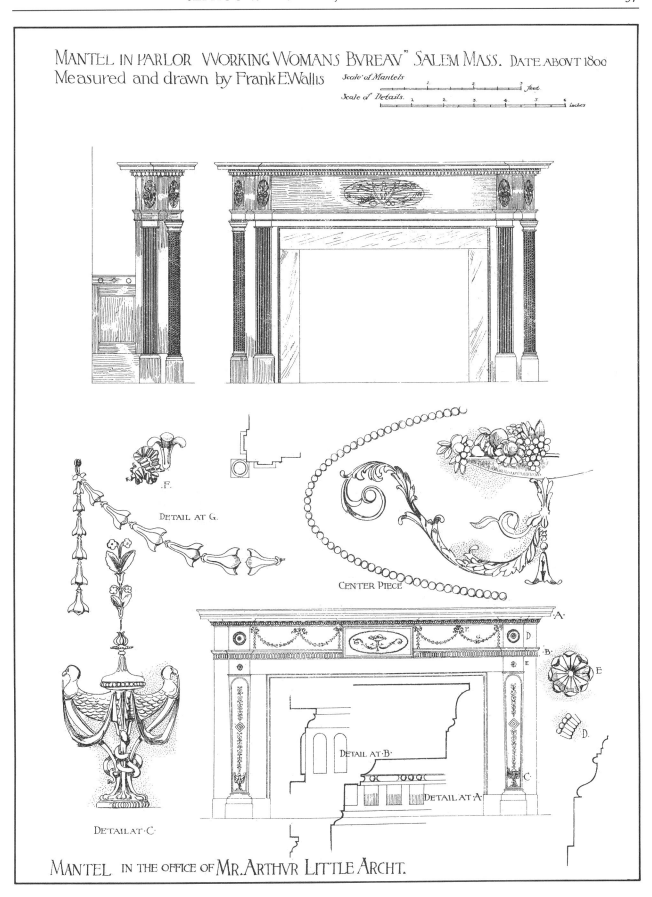

MANTEL IN PARLOR "WORKING WOMANS BVREAV" SALEM MASS. DATE ABOVT 1800
Measured and drawn by Frank E. Wallis

Scale of Mantels
Scale of Details.

.F.

DETAIL AT G.

CENTER PIECE

DETAIL AT B.

DETAIL AT A.

DETAIL AT C.

MANTEL IN THE OFFICE OF MR. ARTHVR LITTLE ARCHT.

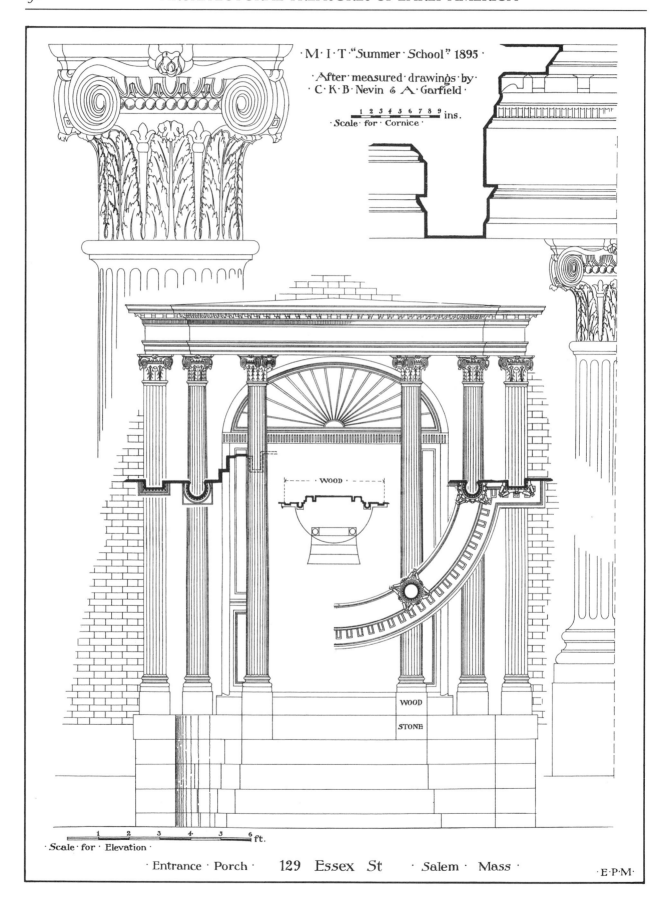

· M · I · T · "Summer · School" · 1895 ·

· After · measured · drawings · by ·
· C · K · B · Nevin · & · A · Garfield ·

1 2 3 4 5 6 7 8 9 ins.
· Scale · for · Cornice ·

· WOOD ·

WOOD

STONE

1 2 3 4 5 6 ft.
· Scale · for · Elevation ·

· Entrance · Porch ·   129 Essex St   · Salem · Mass ·   · E·P·M·

M·I·T· Summer School ·1895·

·After· drawings ·by·H·S·Dutton·
& ·J·F·Gayler·

·Balcony·Rail·

·Balcony·Rail·
0 1 2 3   6   9 in.

·Section· at·B·

bead

·Main· Cornice·
0   3   6   12 in.

bead

dentils

·Section·at· ·A·

·Porch· Cornice·
0   4   6   12 in.

bead

·Cornice· C·
0 1 2 3 4   8 in.

C
fluted   fluted
A   B
D

·FORRESTER· HOUSE·
SALEM, MASS.
·Built·in·1801·

0 3 6 9 12"   2   3   4 ft.

·Section·at·D·
0   1   2   3   4   5 in.

Scale·for·Sections A·B·D·

·Front· Elevatin·
0   5   10   15   20 25 ft.

·Railing· in·rear·
0   1   2   3   4 ft.

·J·C·H·

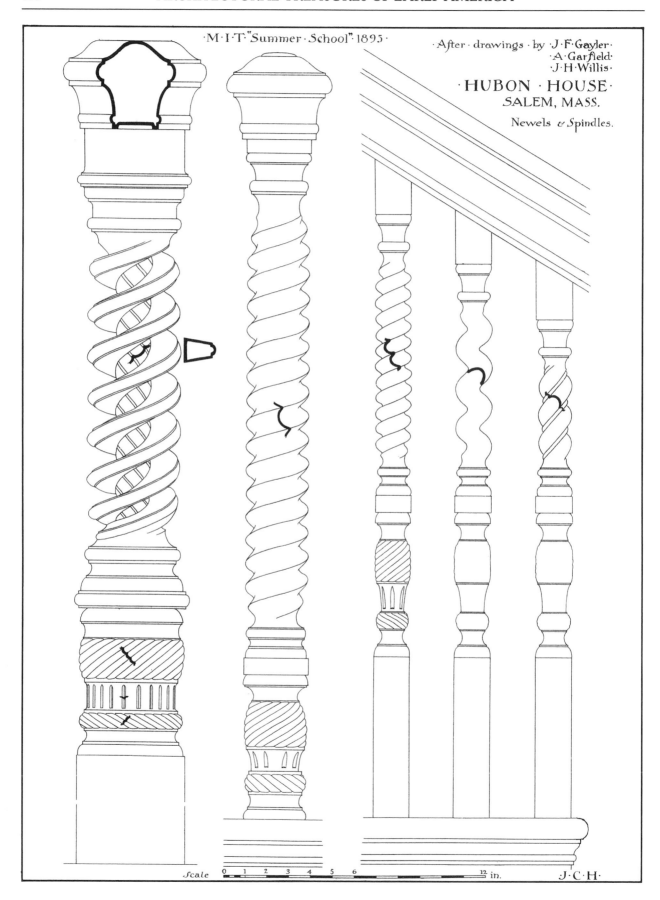

·M·I·T·"Summer·School"·1895·

·After·drawings·by ·J·F·Gayler·
·A·Garfield·
·J·H·Willis·

·HUBON · HOUSE·
SALEM, MASS.

Newels & Spindles.

Scale 0 1 2 3 4 5 6 12 in.

J·C·H·

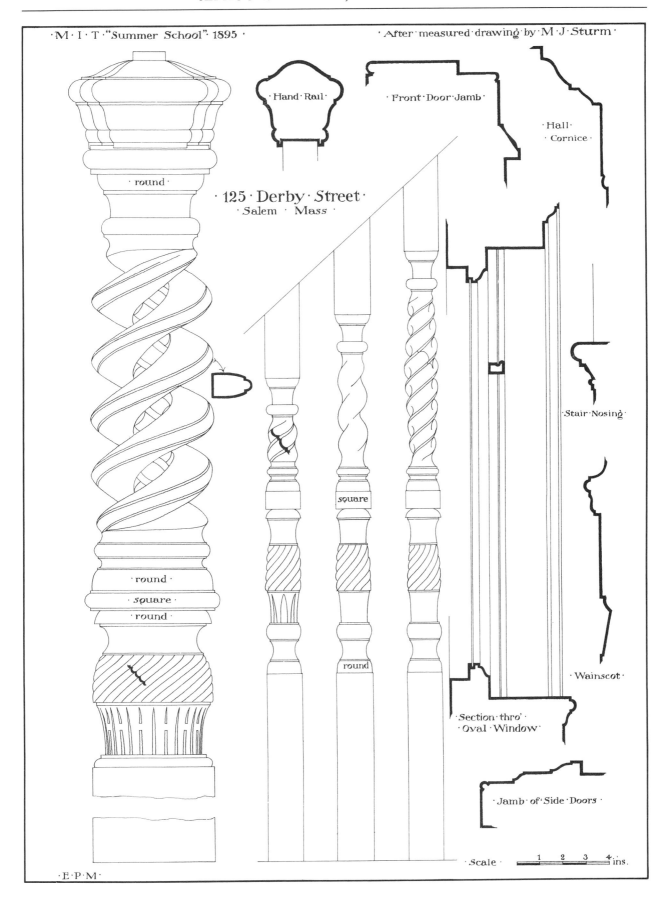

·M · I · T ·"Summer School". 1895 ·

· After · measured · drawing · by · M · J · Sturm ·

· Hand · Rail ·

· Front · Door · Jamb ·

· Hall · Cornice ·

· round ·

· 125 · Derby · Street ·
· Salem · Mass ·

· Stair · Nosing ·

square

round ·
· square ·
· round ·

round

· Wainscot ·

· Section · thro' ·
· Oval · Window ·

· Jamb · of · Side · Doors ·

· Scale ·   1   2   3   4 · ins.

·E·P·M·

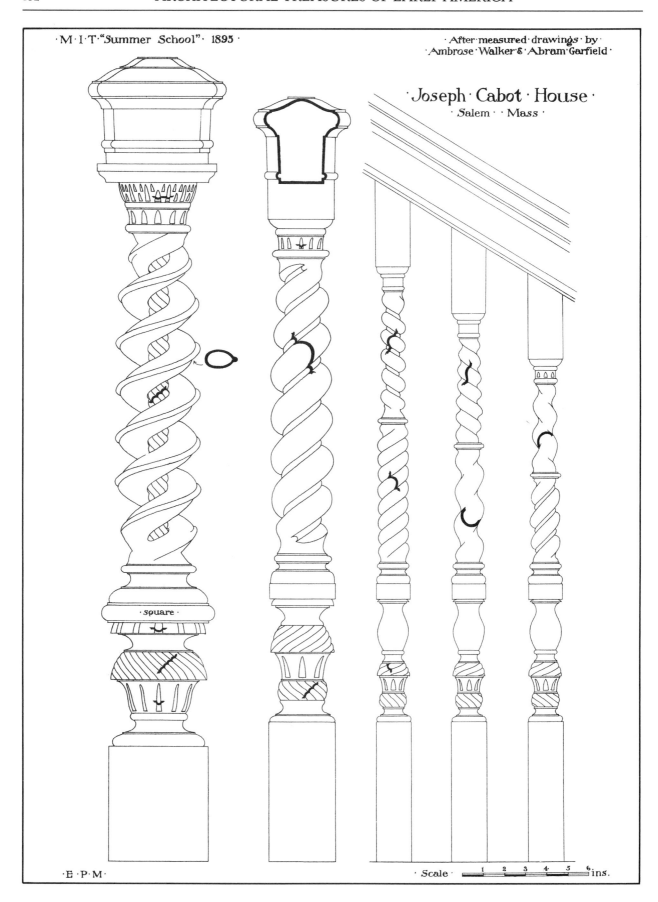

·M·I·T·"Summer School"· 1895·

·After·measured·drawings·by·
·Ambrose·Walker·&·Abram·Garfield·

·Joseph·Cabot·House·
·Salem·· Mass·

·square·

·E·P·M·

·Scale·   1   2   3   4   5   6·ins.

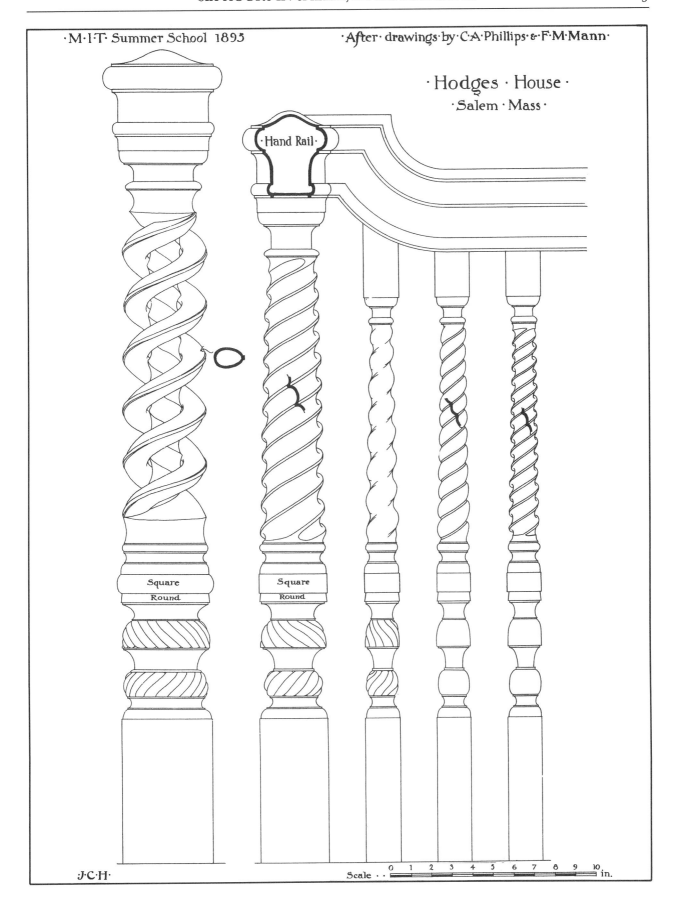

·M·I·T· Summer School 1895

·After· drawings ·by· C·A·Phillips·&·F·M·Mann·

·Hodges · House ·
·Salem · Mass·

·Hand Rail·

Square
Round

Square
Round

Scale · · 0 1 2 3 4 5 6 7 8 9 10 in.

J·C·H·

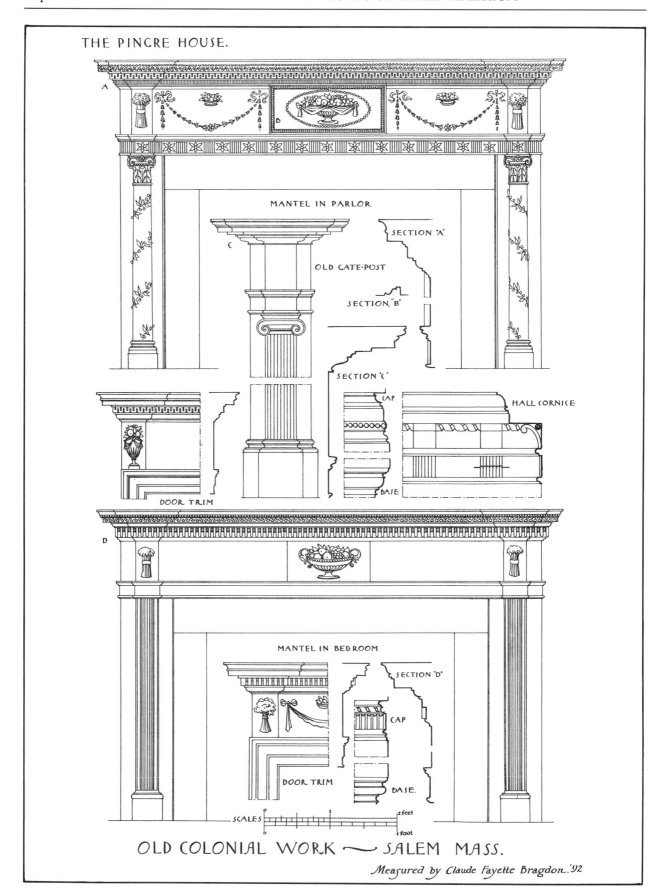

THE PINCRE HOUSE.

MANTEL IN PARLOR

SECTION "A"

OLD GATE-POST

SECTION "B"

SECTION "C"

CAP

HALL CORNICE

DASE

DOOR TRIM

MANTEL IN BEDROOM

SECTION "D"

CAP

DOOR TRIM

DASE.

SCALES   2 feet   1 foot

OLD COLONIAL WORK — SALEM MASS.

Measured by Claude Fayette Bragdon. '92

THE CUSTOM HOUSE

WINDOW IN SECOND STORY HALL

FRONT ENTRANCE

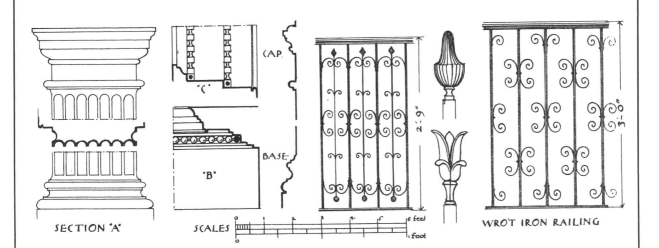

SECTION "A"   SCALES   WRO'T IRON RAILING

CAP.

"C"

BASE

"B"

OLD COLONIAL WORK ~ SALEM, MASS.

Measured by Claude Fayette Bragdon 92

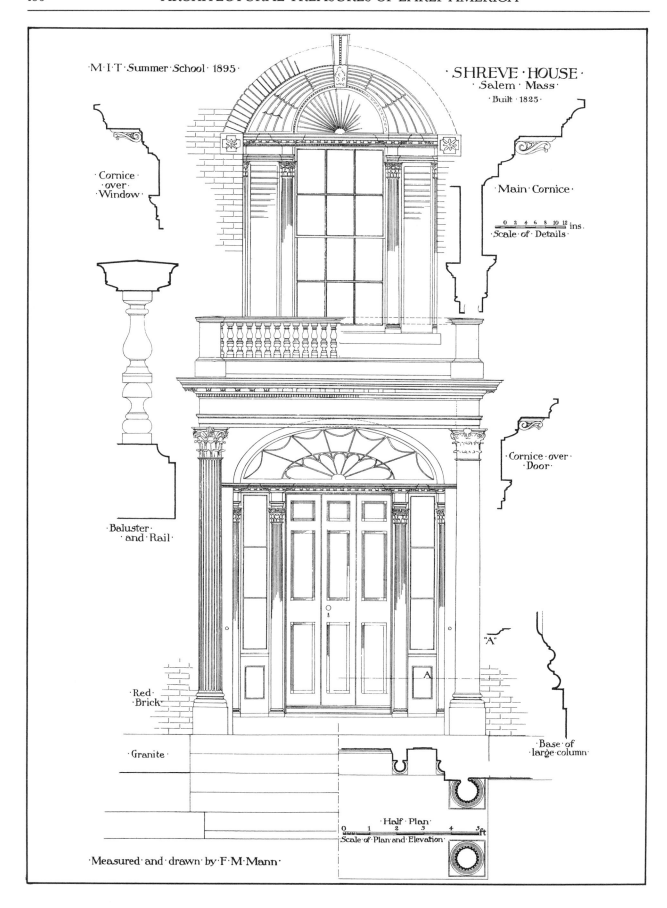

·M·I·T· Summer·School· 1895·

·SHREVE· HOUSE·
· Salem· Mass·
· Built ·1825·

· Cornice ·
· over ·
· Window ·

· Main· Cornice ·

0 2 4 6 8 10 12 ·ins·
·Scale· of· Details·

· Cornice· over·
· Door ·

· Baluster ·
· and· Rail ·

"A"

A

· Red ·
· Brick ·

· Base· of ·
· large· column ·

· Granite ·

· Half· Plan ·
0   1   2   3   4   5·ft·
·Scale· of· Plan· and· Elevation·

· Measured· and· drawn· by· F·M·Mann·

Detail at H.

Detail at A.

34 Chestnut St.

Detail at B.

Detail at F.

Detail at G.

Detail at C.

25 Chestnut St.

Federal St.   Federal St.   Lafayette St.

0 1 2 3 4 5 6 7 8 9 10 11 12 inches.
Scale of Details.

GATE POSTS · SALEM MASS.

Measured and drawn by Frank E. Wallis.

Scale 0 3 6 9 12 in. 1   2   3   4   5   6 feet.

Detail at E.
Gen. Oliver's House.

Washington Sq.

Detail at D.

Supposed to have been designed by McIntire, Arch't. early in this Century.

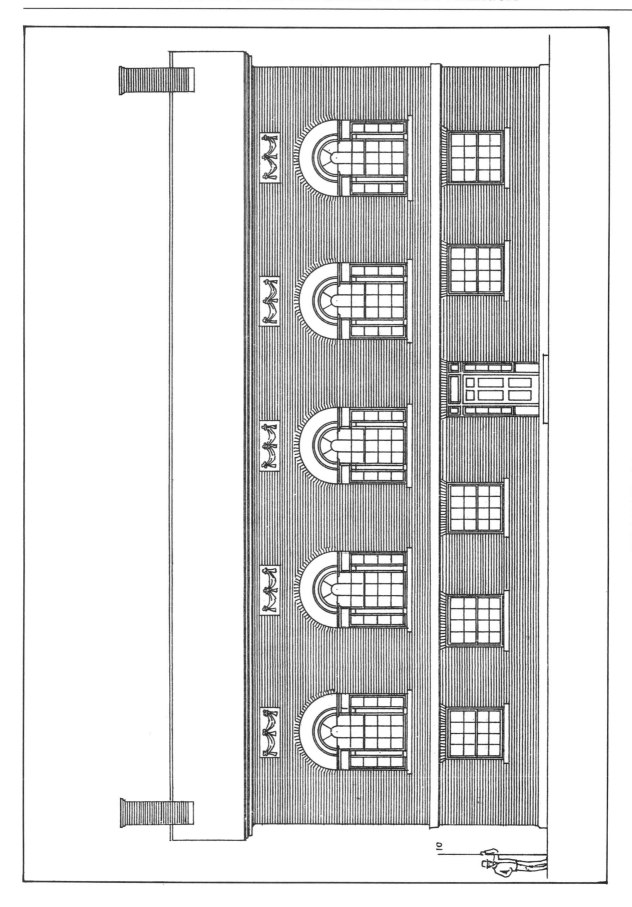

HAMILTON HALL, SALEM, MASSACHUSETTS

Georgian Houses
of New England

Text by
Robert S. Peabody
Originally published in 1901 as
Volume II of The Georgian Period

Front Porch
WILLIAMS HOUSE — 1808 — 1234 WASHINGTON STREET, BOSTON, MASSACHUSETTS

THE GEORGIAN HOUSES OF NEW ENGLAND[1]

IN England, during the last fifty years, one historical style after another has found favor with architects and their clients. The *Vitruvius Britannicus* shows what a hold Palladian design had on that country. The Houses of Parliament and the new Law Courts indicate quite different tendencies in the public taste. Between these extremes there were many other "periods" that had their followers and when fashion turned for models to the time of Queen Anne and the Georges there was at least one strong argument to support the movement. It was truly asserted that this period was the latest one during which art as applied to building was indigenous, or at least well understood by the craftsmen who used it. The modern lovers of this style hoped to bring back something of this simple and happy condition.

The buildings that came of these endeavors certainly have a familiar and cosy charm. In the homely work of the time of the Georges architects found walls of red brick and white mortar, tiled roofs, white doors and sashes, and well-studied Classical finish in wood and plaster within and without the house. They used the same means in new work, and their buildings, though supplied with comforts that even Thackeray himself did not dream of, would yet have seemed as familiar and homelike to him and to his heroes as they do to us.

In America we, too, have had successive revivals of historical architecture, and back of these we now see there was a time when, in the days of the Georges, all our mechanics used one simple, refined and beautiful style of detail. Many a choice wooden cornice, many a stiff wooden mantel in our farmhouses attest this. "Plancia," "fascia" and "soffit" still are Yankee words in spite of our periods of revival. In short we now have discovered that we, too, have had an artistic past worthy of study.

Put our heirlooms—any old material we have—into a mediaeval room, and they will be more or less out of keeping. In fact, with the successive fashions that in recent years have swept over the country, we have to build, not new houses alone, but all their furnishings to match. It would be worth while for us to remember that our heirlooms are tall clocks Copley or Stuart portraits, convex mirrors, ancient chests and drawers, bits of carving perhaps by Gibbons, Paul Revere tankards or andirons, brass candlesticks, and chairs that came over in the *Mayflower*. We think with interest of the parish glebes of Cambridge and Portsmouth, of the old Tories' Row in Cambridge. Many are the old wainscoted rooms for which we have an affectionate remembrance; the staircases with boxed steps with a rich scroll under each box, and with the varied balusters carved into a twist by hand; the great brick chimney-corners with Dutch tile borders, and crane, pot-hooks and trammels, and hanging kettles, and the yawning flues resting on oak mantel-bars and opening a clear road to the stars above. Whenever we see these interiors we, too want to live amid wainscoting nestle in elliptical-arched nooks, and warm ourselves beneath the high mantels a blazing wood fires. We want to see our old chairs and pictures thus appropriately en-

[1] Although some of the houses here mentioned have disappeared since this paper, now carefully revised, was published in the *American Architect,* it has seemed worthwhile to speak of them as existing, since they are still so well remembered.

CHRIST CHURCH (OLD NORTH
CHURCH)—1723—BOSTON, MASSACHUSETTS

vironed. We want to go up to bed over boxed stairs
guarded by ramped rails and twisted balusters. In
short, in this Colonial work we find delicacy, grace and
picturesqueness, and, combined with it, a familiar
aspect, and a fitness to harmonize with all those heirlooms and old possessions which might be put to
shame by other fashions.

Though most of our models are of the Georgian
period here and there one can be found of an earlier
date. We have our Charles River, our Cape Ann, our
Queen Anne's Corner, and some houses, also of early
date. The Cradock mansion was built in the day of
Charles the First; the Fairbanks House in Dedham,
and the Curtis House in Jamaica Plain, during the
Commonwealth; and these are still occupied by the
families of their builders. The Province House[2] is of
the time of Charles II; the Sudbury Inn of James II;
the Batchelder House in Cambridge dates from William and Mary; the Old Corner Bookstore from Queen
Anne; while the President's house and Massachusetts
Hall at Cambridge, and the Adams (once Vassall)

House at Quincy, all date from the reign of George
the First. These are representative houses; but yet the
richest and finest models we have date from between
1727 and 1760, when George II reigned: Peperell House
in Kittery, 1730; Hancock House[2], 1737; Royall House,
Medford, 1738; Holden Chapel, Cambridge, 1745;
Wells mansion, Cambridge, 1745; Wentworth House,
Little Harbor, 1750; Longfellow (Vassall) House, 1759;
Ladd House, Portsmouth, 1764.

If we study these Colonial buildings, we see nearly
all the early work in this neighborhood roofed with
steep-pitched gable roofs. Rare instances occur like the
stone Cradock house at Medford, where the gambrel
roof appears earlier; but from 1686, the date of the
Sudbury Inn, to 1737, the date of the Hancock House,
the gambrel roof is common. Later it became frequent
to pitch the roof in from all sides to a ridge or to a
second pitch surrounded by a balustrade, and it is
under such roofs that the richest interiors of our neighborhood are still found; such as the Longfellow and
Wells and Riedesel houses in Cambridge, the Ladd
and Langdon at Portsmouth, the Winslow at Plymouth, the Lee at Marblehead.

Thus it appears that the gambrel roof is typical of
but one period of Colonial work. Where did it come
from? Though now and then something like it is seen
in England, it certainly is not characteristic of England. It is said that the bricks of Peter Sergeant's
house, afterwards the Province House, were brought
from Holland; and it is at about that date that the
gambrel roof became prevalent. Possibly it is a remi-
niscence of Holland, but whether by way of England
or of New York, it would be hard now to say. The later
and richer mansions were large and square, and with
so little detail outside that until in recent times, when
our builders learned to give a texture or tone that
emulates the effect of age, they feared to imitate these
plain, angular and box-like forms—but now, as the
"Colonial House" is possessing the land, we, in turn,
long for the thin, sparse details of the early models.

But severity of form is by no means a characteristic
of all Colonial work. The old Fairbanks House at Dedham, part of which is of early date with high-pitched
roof, and part later, with a gambrel roof, forms a most
picturesque pile; and so does the scattered house at
Little Harbor, with gables at different heights and
floors at different levels, and with a council-chamber
wing that runs off from the main building at an un-
called-for angle that would delight Mr. Norman Shaw.
Again, among the gambrel roofs, the great lumbering
Sudbury Inn, with its wide-spread barns and out-
houses, forms a most hospitable group, and the gables
of the Goodman cottage at Lenox, low, broad and
cosy, twinkle their many-eyed sashes over the lilac

[2]Now destroyed.

CHRIST CHURCH — 1761 — CAMBRIDGE,
MASSACHUSETTS
Peter Harrison, Architect

THE WAYSIDE INN—1686—SUDBURY,
MASSACHUSETTS

hedges of the forecourt as the traveler passes through that lovely Berkshire[3] country. These all show us that a picturesque group of any sort is not incongruous with the style.

It is not because we have no public buildings that I have dwelt on the Colonial mansions. The Old North Church and the King's Chapel, the Old State House, the Newport State House, and the Old Ship Meeting House at Hingham are all excellent buildings. Simple though some of them are, they all have style and elegance, and they may properly furnish inspiration to those who are to design modern buildings for similar uses in those ancient neighborhoods.

The chief beauties of the detail in all our Colonial work lie in its disciplined and almost universal refinement and dignity, and, even when display is attempted, in the absence of vulgarity or eccentricity. Then, too, we find Classical detail everywhere used as the common language of every carpenter, and treated freely with regard only for comfort, cosiness or stateliness, and without a too superstitious reverence for Pal-

---

[3] Of the Judge Walker House, the present owner of the house, Robert C. Rockwell, Esq., writes:—

"This house was built in 1804 by Judge William Walker, of Lenox, for his son, Judge William Perrin Walker. Judge Rockwell married the eldest daughter of the latter. The elder Judge Walker was in early life a carpenter and builder, and probably this house was built under his immediate supervision. About the same time he built a companion house, of smaller size, at Lenox Furnace (the present Lenox Dale) for his daughter, the wife of Dr. Charles Worthington.

"The house at Lenox stands upon land known as the 'Ministers' Grant,' which was granted by the Province in 1739 to Ephraim Williams and others, as compensation for certain lands in Stockbridge given up for the use of the Indian Mission. In the division of the 'Ministers' Grant' in 1741, this land was set off to Jonathan Edwards, the elder. Judge Walker bought the house site in 1803, and built the house as above stated."

ladio or Scamozzi. Hence arose a pure and harmonious style, and one naturally inquires whence the information of the old builders came, and whether tradition and copying, as in mediaeval times, could have led to such a varied use of Italian *motifs*, or whether for these Colonial carpenters there was some more definite source of instruction.

The English mansions, which Nash and Richardson have sketched for us so thoroughly, were of an earlier period than the building days in our country. Longleat, Hatfield, Holland House, and many of those structures which, like Longleat were built under Italian care, or, like the others, bore a more or less Italian detail on their mediaeval forms, date from about the time when the Pilgrims landed at Plymouth. Steep gables vie with pediments in these compositions, and mullions and pointed arches stand side by side with the orders. Of such work no examples of moment were raised on our shores, for it was doubtless long before buildings of any pretension were required by a struggling people. But this was not the case with movable objects, and this Jacobean period has been well handed down to us in the many pieces of furniture brought over or made by the early colonists. As is well known, the chairs reputed to have come over in the *Mayflower* might have laden a fleet, and the New England family that does not possess one or more has feeble claim to aristocratic pretension. The bulbous legs and posts, the ill-formed pediments, and the other details of this period, appeared however, in our country, in these works alone.

But meanwhile Inigo Jones made his two visits to Italy, and, full of enthusiasm for Palladio's work, made his designs in a more purely Italian manner,

OLD CORNER BOOKSTORE—C1712—BOSTON,
MASSACHUSETTS

CURTIS HOUSE — 1639 — JAMAICA PLAIN,
MASSACHUSETTS

with well-understood detail. He even added an Italian portico to the noble mediaeval Cathedral of St. Paul. When he died in 1652, Sir Christopher Wren monopolized all the important English practice, working always with much regard for group and line, and mechanical skill, but with far less care for detail than his predecessor. In his turn, in 1723, Sir Christopher Wren died. Vanbrugh, Hawksmoor, Gibbs, Campbell, Taylor, Adam, Chambers, such are the more or less familiar names of those whose work occupied the rest of the century; and the period when our Colonial work was rich and interesting is thus included between the lives of Jones and Chambers. Their taste is often reflected in the buildings of this time, which indeed may have been sometimes of their own designing.

It was the period of rule and method; of aliquot parts, modules, and minutes. True, this discipline was confined to details; for, as in the case of the exteriors of the houses, the floor plans admitted very varied and picturesque effects which principally regarded the stairs. At the Holmes House [now replaced by the Hemenway Gymnasium] and Longfellow House in Cambridge, the front and rear stairs start from opposite ends of the house, and separate again after meeting on a common landing. At the Ladd House and at one other house in Portsmouth, the stairs wind up in different manners in the corner of the larger hall. At the Winslow House in Plymouth, the stair-landing crosses the door-opening, and the portion left open above the landing is filled-in with twisted balusters.

Concerning the Winslow House, Mr. J. Everett Chandler, architect, of Boston, writes of our illustrations, on pages 119 and 154 as follows: —

"The print is a representation of the entrance to the old Winslow House in Plymouth, probably built about 1755, by a son of Governor Winslow. Several years ago it fell to my lot to extensively remodel and add to the old house for a Chicago gentleman, to be used by him as a summer residence. The house had already been changed greatly in a former remodelling, and the four front rooms, the fine hallway and the exterior door, shown in the print, were the only really old portions of the house left, and these have been kept as much as possible as they were. But, on account of the proximity of the house to two fine old lindens, the house was moved back 30 feet and raised 5 feet. Then the addition of two wings of an area equal to the old house necessitated other changes until the char-

HOLDEN CHAPEL — 1745 — HARVARD
UNIVERSITY, CAMBRIDGE, MASSACHUSETTS

acter of the house became considerably changed, although the finish in the additions, inside and out, was made in the spirit and period of the old — the earliest, strongest, and to my mind the best, period of Colonial work. The doorway has an interesting frieze of turkeys, vines, grapes and flowers — looking like a curious mixture of a copy from old Byzantine work and a piece of old embroidery, very like a piece I found in an old house near by. I kept the door-frame exactly as it was, hoping it would remain so many years, but just as the house was nearing completion my client announced that he must have a covered porch! So I reluctantly added one — copying exactly the archaic-looking Corinthian order, entablature, frieze and all — making an elliptical porch with a domed top: — so the old doorway is still there, although somewhat hidden from sight."

Yet, though picturesque effects add many charms to these interiors, their distinguished and refined character could only come from respect for architectural traditions and studied training in the orders. It will be found that old libraries furnish the clew to all this, much more than might be supposed. The English works alone on architecture which appeared in the last century are very numerous and very carefully prepared. I have found a large copy of Batty Langley's

classical work in an old loft in New Hampshire. I doubt not that such books were common here in the days when our early work was executed, and I think existing mantels, cornices, alcoves, etc., might possibly identified if these books were studied.

Mr. Eastlake, in his *History of the Gothic Revival,* speaks of English works on Classical design by Shute, in 1563, and Sir Henry Wotton, in 1624. These I have not seen; but one can readily see others in our libraries. Gibbs's works, published in 1739, included the engravings of St. Martin's Church in London. Batty and Thomas Langley, besides their Gothic book, which Mr. Eastlake ridicules, also published an excellent Classical work, most of the plates in which are dated 1739. Ware's *Architecture,* which is voluminous, and has many plates of interiors, is dated 1756. Chippendale's book is dated 1762, and gives us furniture in the "most fashionable styles," which were evidently French; and it seems as if Governor Langdon, who built in 1784, or Jeremiah Lee, whose house dates from 1768, had perhaps received a copy of this work before the Louis Quinze curves were cut on their great chimney-pieces at Portsmouth and Marblehead. This same Chippendale, whose chairs and tables, or their copies, are frequent in America, besides affecting a French taste, had a fancy for Chinese work, giving us designs for chairs and railings in the Chinese manner. Chairs of this make are to be seen at Portsmouth. Chippendale thus seems an amusing forerunner to the Queen-Anne-Japanese designer of a recent day. Swan's book follows these others in 1768, with many designs for mantels and other work, and Paine publishes fine plates in 1783; and the third edition of the correct and elegant Sir William Chambers is dated 1791. In 1811 Asher Benjamin published in Charlestown, Massachusetts, the second edition of the *American Builder's Companion,* which contains most of the types of cornices, mantels, and other details to be seen about the houses of that date east of the Connecticut River — such as the Ticknor House on Park Street, the old Franklin Street houses, and the West Boston Church in Boston — and about the same date, on the other side of the water, Thomas Hope published a series of beautiful drawings of furniture, inspired by the discoveries at Spalatro and at Athens, and made familiar to us by the French furniture of the First Empire. Thus Hope foreshadowed the Greek and Roman revivals with which we are familiar.

These books, which are probably but examples of a larger number, indicate how our forefathers obtained their knowledge. They are filled with designs of doors and windows, chimney-pieces, buffets, monuments, clock cases, bustons, girandoles, tables, and chairs. Often the plates are very fine, but they rarely suggest

BUILDING OF THE McLEAN INSANE ASYLUM — c1820 — SOMERVILLE, MASSACHUSETTS
Charles Bulfinch, Architect

the extreme delicacy and fineness of moulding so characteristic of the real work. Curiously enough, however, though ramped rails and turned or carved balusters occur in these books, I have not seen one print of a twisted baluster such as were well-nigh universal in all houses of importance with us at that time. This is not because they were peculiar to this country; indeed, I have supposed ours generally were carved in England, and I well remember almost identical patterns in London. It is strange that they do not appear in the plates, considering that they were the most conspicuous ornament in American work of that time.

Almost all the designing to be seen in these volumes is founded on a study of the orders, which is held throughout as almost synonymous with the study of architecture. Mr. B. Langley thus urges this fact on his hearers: —

"'Tis a Matter of very great Surprise to me, how any person dare presume to discourage others from the Study thereof, and thereby render them very often less serviceable to the Publick than so many Brutes. But to prevent this Infection from diffusing its poisonous Effluvia's any further," he, in short, peremptorily admonishes his readers to understand the five orders of columns, whose general proportions will not escape their memories "after having practised them about half a Dozen Times."

The orders are objects of serious study still throughout the civilized world, and more now in this country than for long past. There is no reason to fear the poisonous effluvia that Mr. Langley deplored in his day. The prospective house-owner may safely hope for a house in a classic style, and, if he wants it homelike also, he can find no better field for suggestions fitted to our usages than among the Georgian mansions of New England.

NOTE: The pages following are a pictorial study of New England architecture and, as such, may encompass styles other than Georgian.

Staircase
MAIN BUILDING — 1818 — McLEAN INSANE ASYLUM, SOMERVILLE, MASSACHUSETTS
Charles Bulfinch, Architect

Stair Hall
WINSLOW HOUSE, PLYMOUTH, MASSACHUSETTS

HOUSE AT LITTLE HARBOR

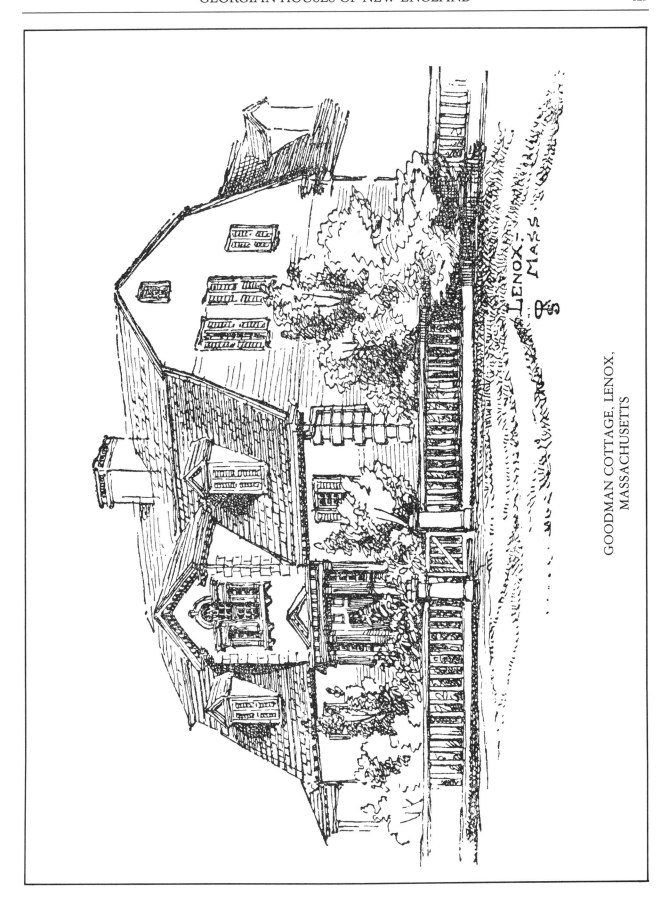

GOODMAN COTTAGE, LENOX,
MASSACHUSETTS

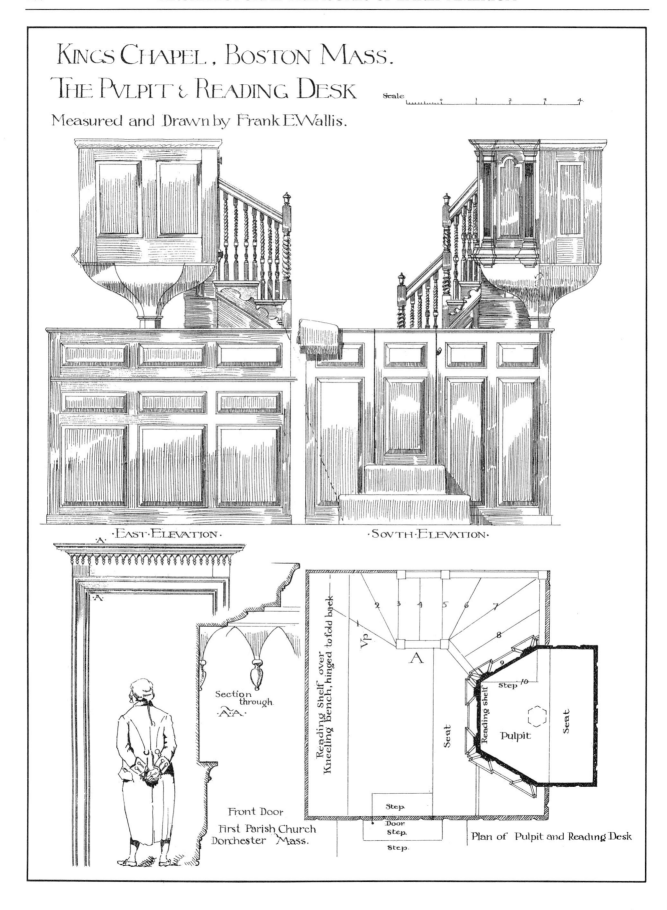

KINGS CHAPEL, BOSTON MASS.
THE PVLPIT & READING DESK

Scale

Measured and Drawn by Frank E. Wallis.

·EAST·ELEVATION·   ·SOVTH·ELEVATION·

·A·

·A·

Section
through
·A·A·

Front Door
First Parish Church
Dorchester Mass.

Reading Shelf over
Kneeling bench, hinged to fold back

Vp

1 2 3 4 5 6 7

8

A

9

Step 10

Reading shelf

Step.

Door
Step.

Step.

Seat

Seat

Pulpit

Plan of Pulpit and Reading Desk

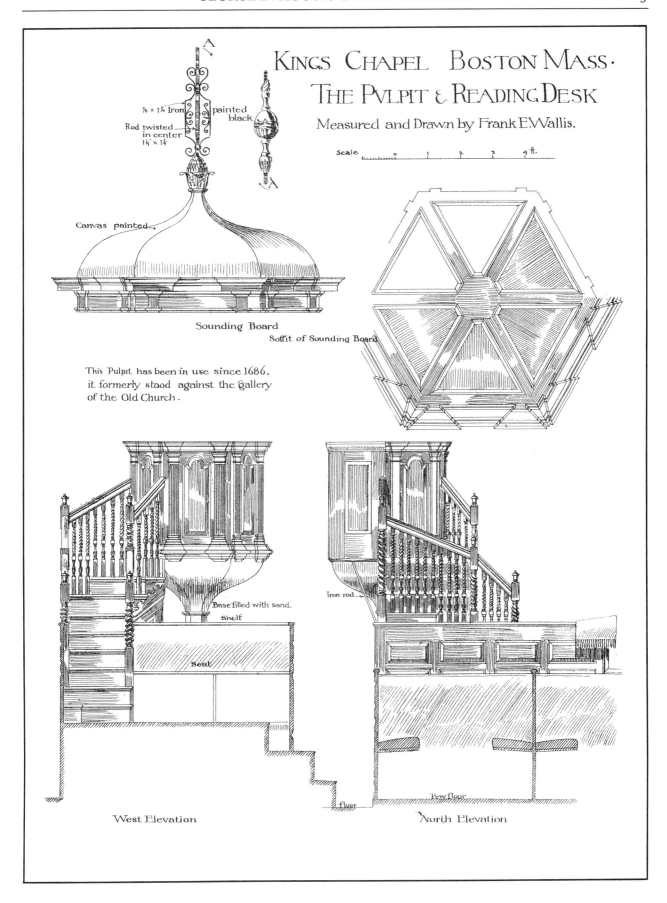

A

¾ × 1¼ Iron   painted black

Rod twisted in center 1½ × 1¼

A

Canvas painted

KINGS CHAPEL BOSTON MASS·
THE PVLPIT & READING DESK

Measured and Drawn by Frank E. Wallis.

Scale   0   1   2   3   4 ft.

Sounding Board

Soffit of Sounding Board

This Pulpit has been in use since 1686,
it formerly stood against the gallery
of the Old Church.

Base filled with sand.
Shelf

Iron rod

Seat

West Elevation

floor

Pew floor

North Elevation

27 Church St,
Newport, R.I.

Measured and drawn
by P. G. Gulbranson
1 8 9 4

Entrance
STARKWEATHER HOUSE, PAWTUCKET, RHODE ISLAND

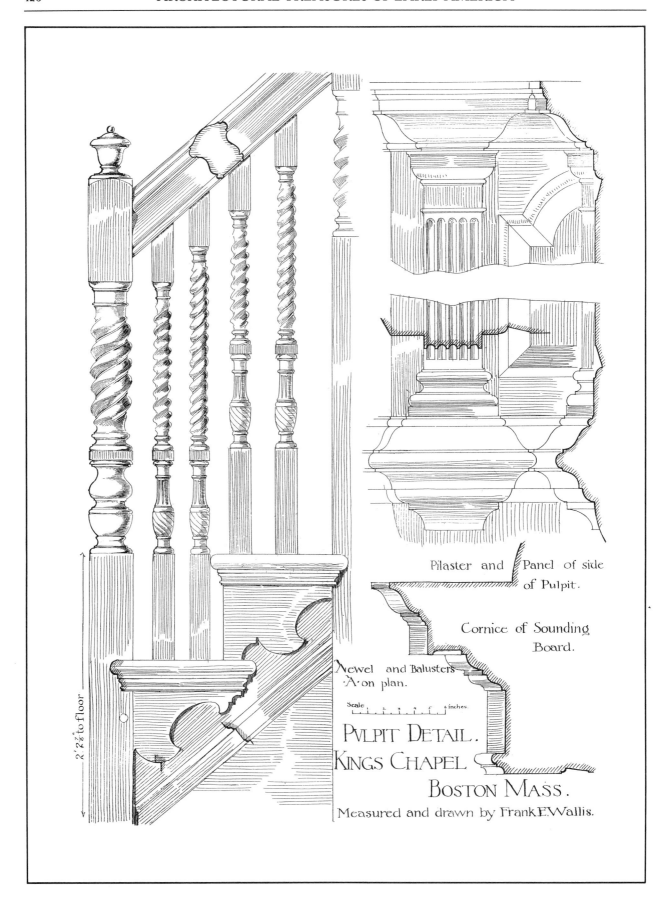

2'2⅞" to floor

Pilaster and Panel of side
of Pulpit.

Cornice of Sounding
Board.

Newel and Balusters
·A· on plan.

Scale

PVLPIT DETAIL.
KINGS CHAPEL
BOSTON MASS.

Measured and drawn by Frank E. Wallis.

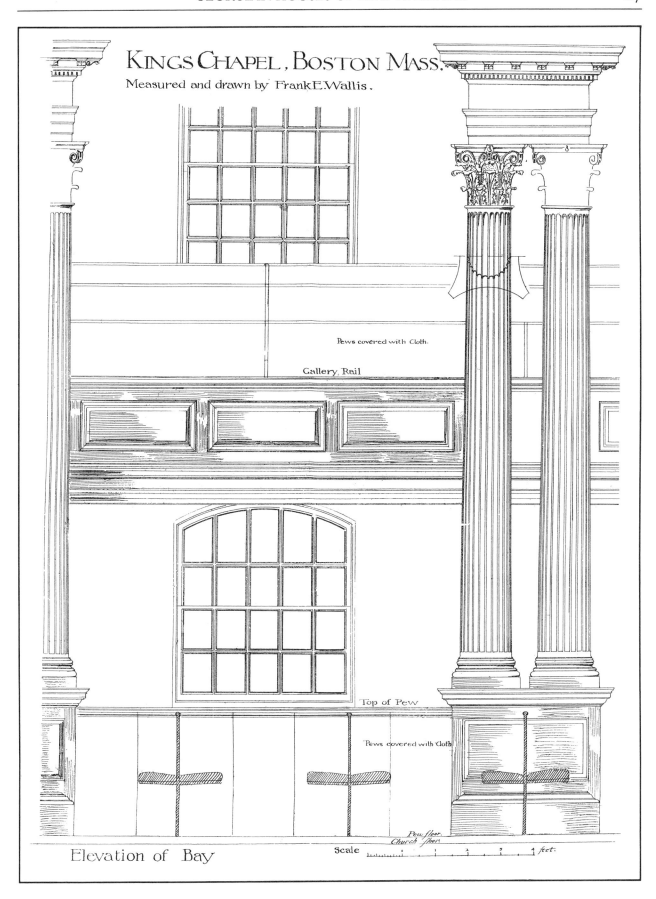

KINGS CHAPEL, BOSTON MASS.

Measured and drawn by Frank E. Wallis.

Pews covered with Cloth.

Gallery Rail

Top of Pew

Pews covered with Cloth

Pew floor.
Church floor.

Elevation of Bay

Scale | | | | | | | | | | 1 | 2 | 3 | 4 feet.

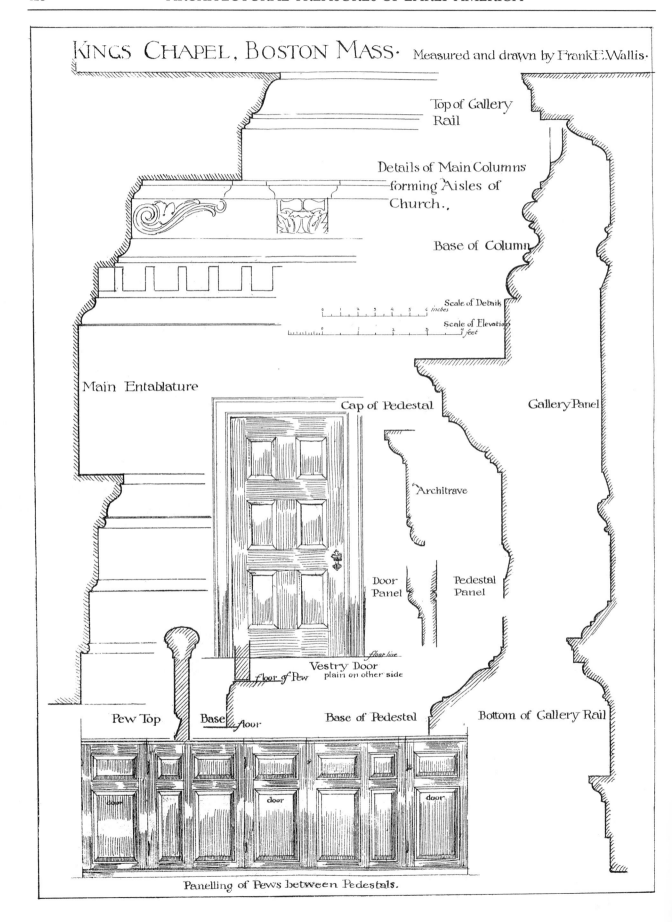

Kings Chapel, Boston Mass· Measured and drawn by Frank E. Wallis·

Top of Gallery Rail

Details of Main Columns forming Aisles of Church·.

Base of Column

Scale of Detail

Scale of Elevation

Main Entablature

Cap of Pedestal

Gallery Panel

Architrave

Door Panel

Pedestal Panel

floor line

Vestry Door
plain on other side

floor of Pew

Pew Top   Base   floor   Base of Pedestal   Bottom of Gallery Rail

door   door   door

Panelling of Pews between Pedestals.

KINGS CHAPEL, BOSTON MASS. Meafured and Drawn by Frank F. Wallis.

Front

End

Plan

Front

Side

Plan

this part of
Rail painted
dark

Scale of Details

Detail of
Communion Table

wooden pins

Scale of Elevations

Communion Table and Two Chairs,
have been in use since 1686
supposed to have been brought over in
Table painted white ... Mayflower.
Chairs Mahogany.

·Chancel·Furniture·

wooden pin

Scale of Key

Key and Tag found
by Sexton, on the top of an old Tomb
in Basement.

floor line

stained
dark.

KingsChapel

Detail of Altar Rail

floor of Chancel

Gate at Altar Rail

Step

floor line

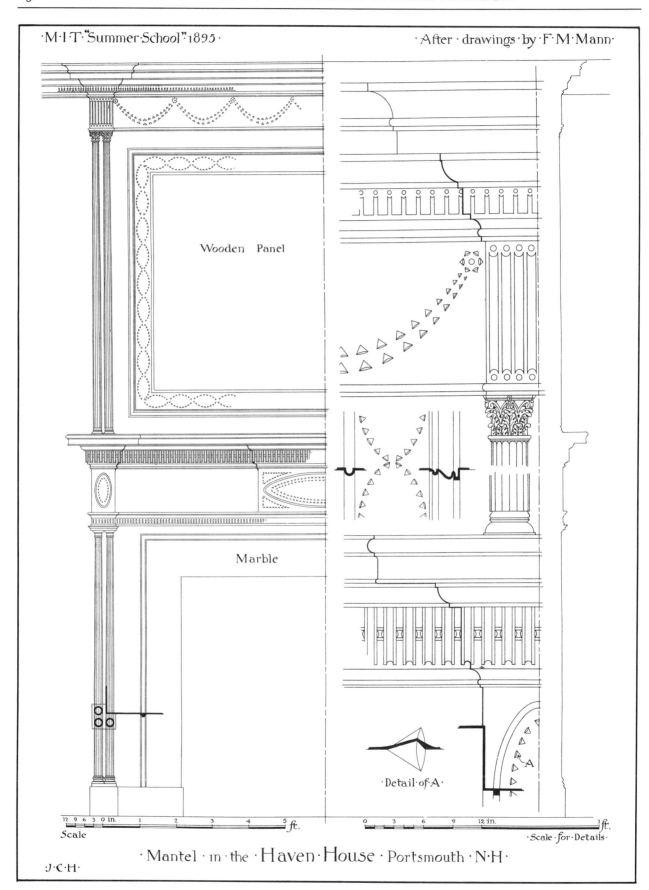

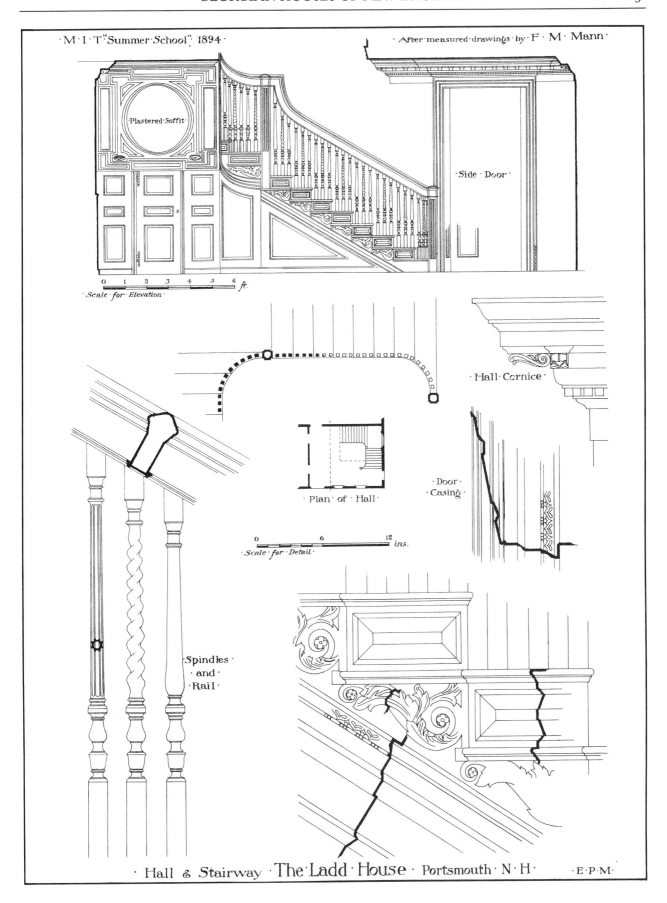

·M·I·T "Summer·School"· 1894 ·

·After·measured·drawings·by·F·M·Mann·

·Plastered·Soffit·

·Side·Door·

0 1 2 3 4 5 6 ft.
·Scale · for · Elevation ·

·Hall·Cornice·

·Plan· of · Hall ·

·Door·
·Casing·

0   6   12 ins.
·Scale · for · Detail ·

·Spindles·
·and·
·Rail·

· Hall & Stairway · The·Ladd·House · Portsmouth · N·H ·   ·E·P·M·

The Pulpit in "The Old Meeting House"
Sandown, N.H.
Measured and Drawn by J A Lane.

Sounding Board.

Plan of Pulpit.

A.   E.

B.   F.

C.

D.   Profiles.

Scales,—

Elevation

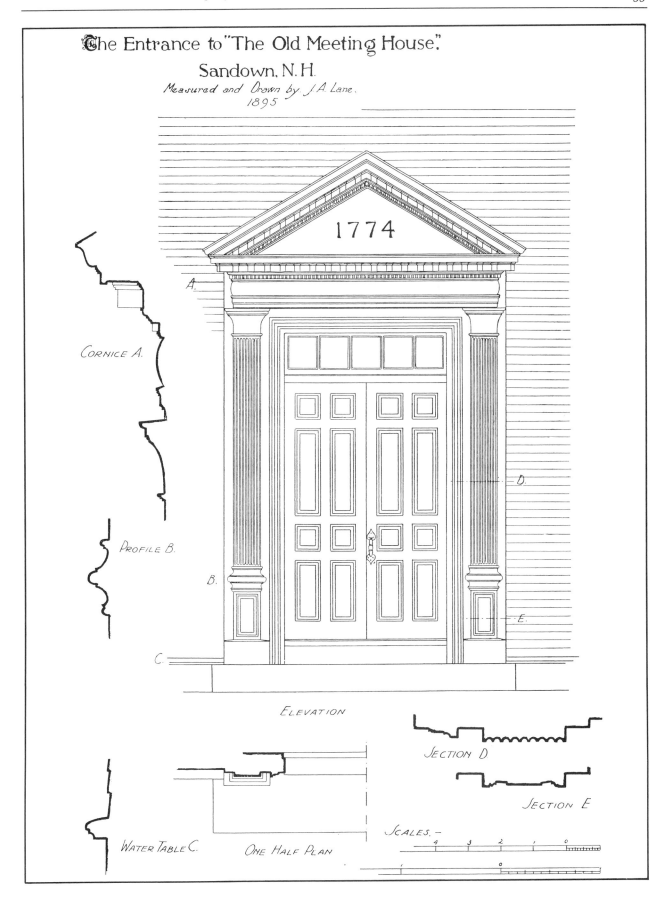

The Entrance to "The Old Meeting House".
Sandown, N.H.
Measured and Drawn by J. A. Lane.
1895

1774

CORNICE A.

PROFILE B.

A.

B.

C.

D.

E.

ELEVATION

WATER TABLE C.

ONE HALF PLAN

SECTION D

SECTION E

SCALES. —

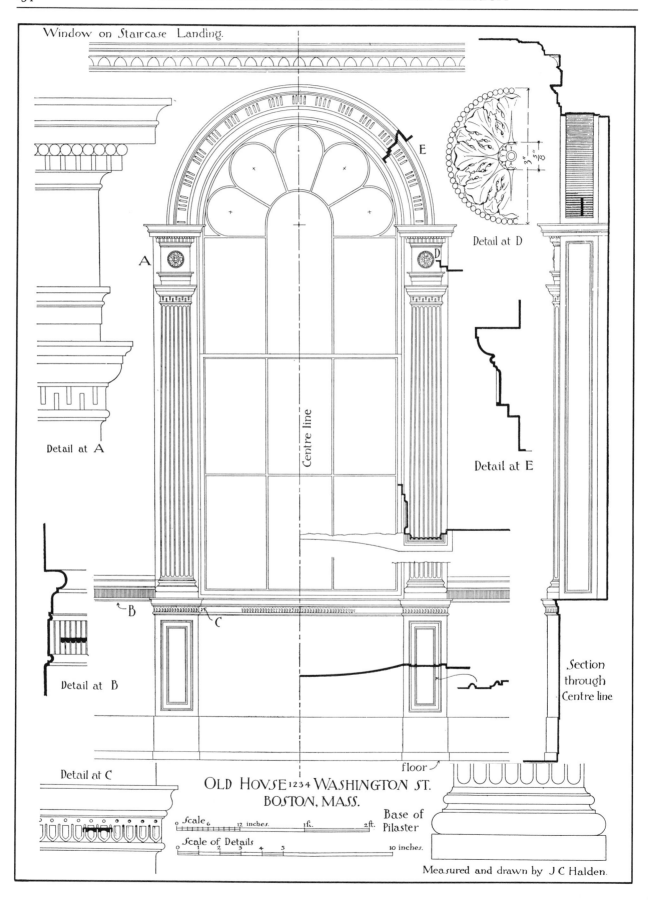

Window on Staircase Landing.

E

Detail at D

Detail at A

A

Centre line

D

Detail at E

B

C

Detail at B

Section through Centre line

Detail at C

floor

OLD HOUSE 1234 WASHINGTON ST.
BOSTON, MASS.

Base of Pilaster

Scale   6   12 inches.   1ft.   2ft.

Scale of Details
0 1 2 3 4 5   10 inches.

Measured and drawn by J C Halden.

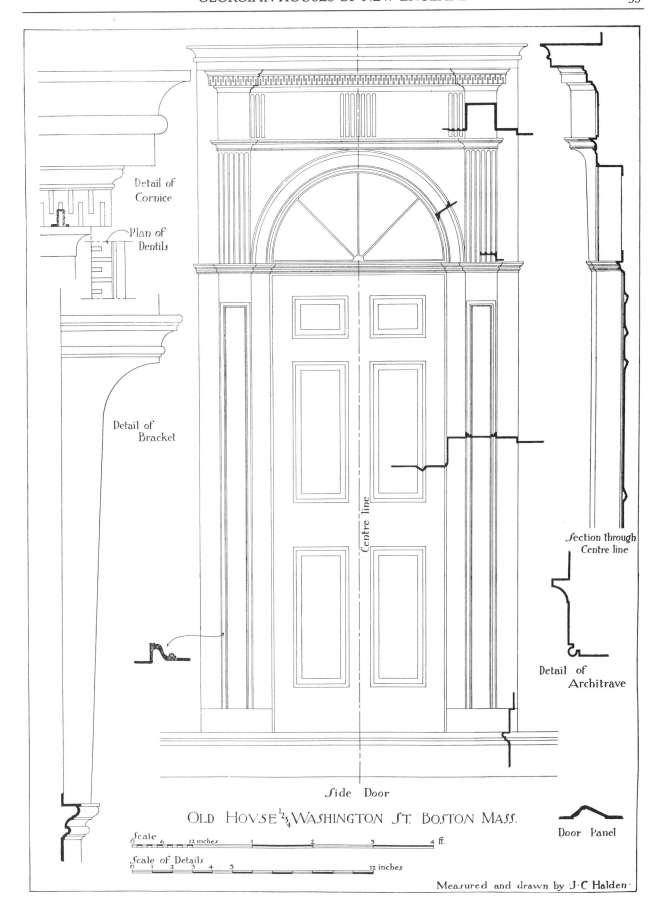

Detail of
Cornice

Plan of
Dentils

Detail of
Bracket

Centre line

Section through
Centre line

Detail of
Architrave

Door Panel

Side Door

OLD HOVSE 1¾ WASHINGTON ST. BOSTON MASS.

Scale
0   6   12 inches   1   2   3   4 ft.

Scale of Details
0 1 2 3 4 5   12 inches

Measured and drawn by J·C·Halden·

Scale of Details

DETAILS OF CORNICE

DETAIL AT B

DETAIL AT A

DETAIL OF BASE

SECTION THROUGH OVERHANG

SECTION

CENTER LINE

PLAN AT A
LOOKING UP

DOOR JAMB

Scale
0 1 2 3 4 5 6 7 8 9 10 11 12 inches. 1 ft. 2 ft.

OLD HOUSE 1234 WASHINGTON ST. BOSTON. MASS.
FRONT ENTRANCE

Measured and drawn
by W Campbell

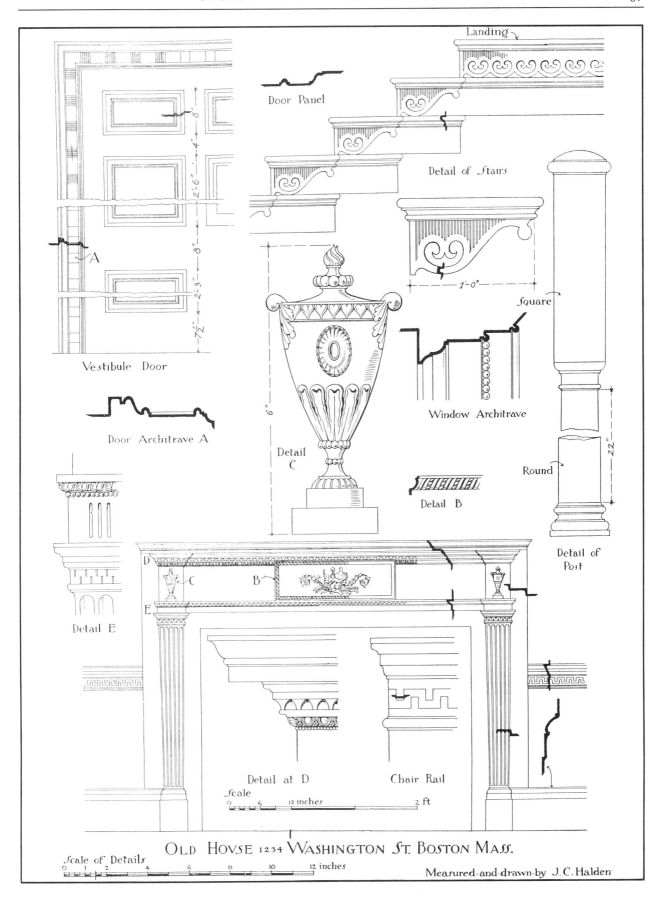

Landing

Door Panel

Detail of Stairs

8"
4"
2'-6"

8"
2'-3"
7½"

A

Vestibule Door

Door Architrave A

Square

1'-0"

Window Architrave

Round

22"

Detail
C

6"

Detail B

Detail of
Post

Detail E

D
C
B
E

Detail at D   Chair Rail

Scale
0   6   12 inches   2 ft

OLD HOVSE 1234 WASHINGTON ST. BOSTON MASS.

Scale of Details
0 1 2   4   6   8   10   12 inches

Measured and drawn by J.C. Halden

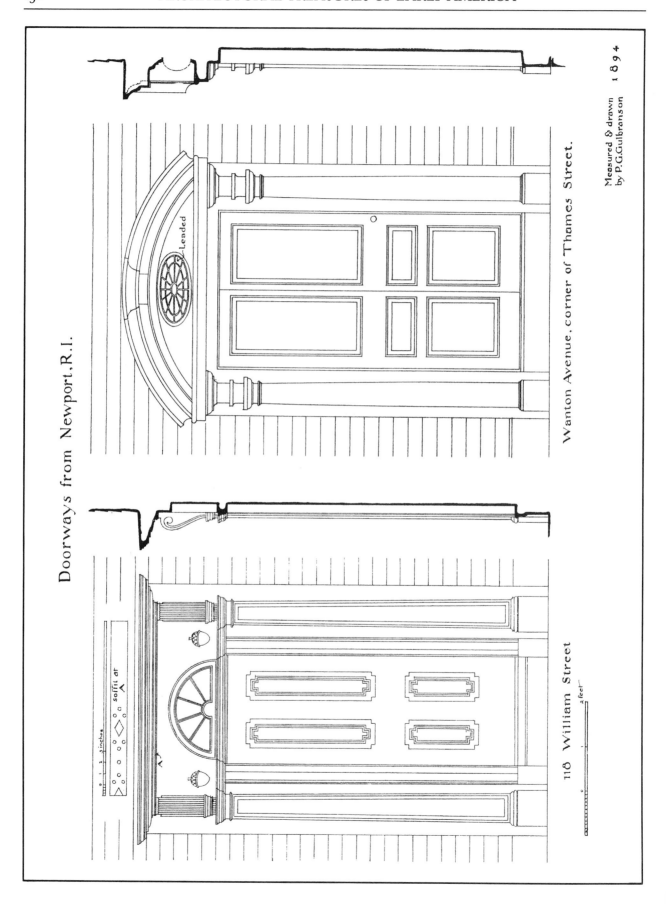

Doorways from Newport, R.I.

Wanton Avenue, corner of Thames Street.

118 William Street

Measured & drawn
by P.G.Gulbranson

1894

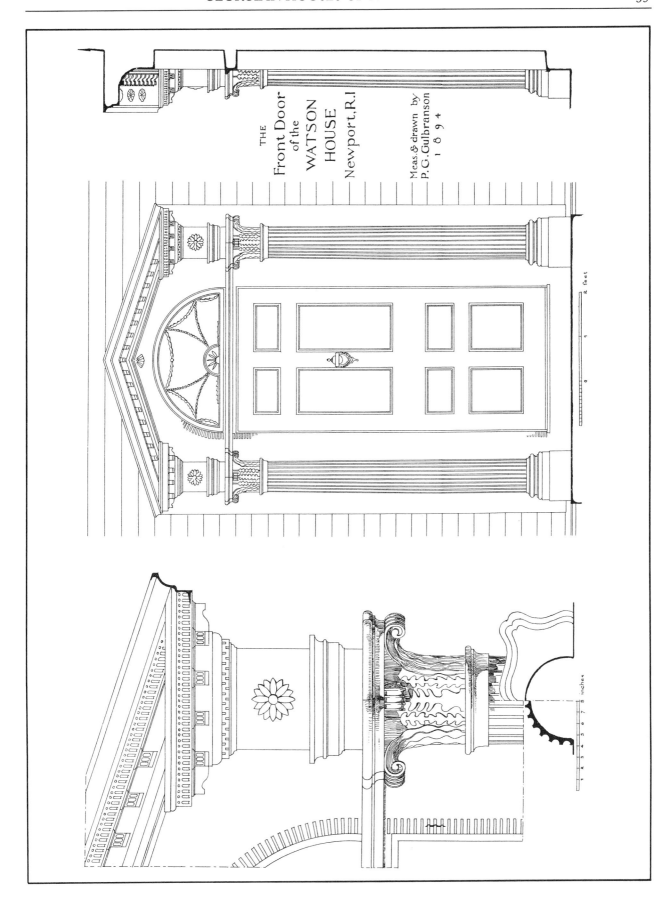

THE
Front Door
of the
WATSON
HOUSE
Newport, R.I

Meas. & drawn by
P.C. Gulbranson
1 8 9 4

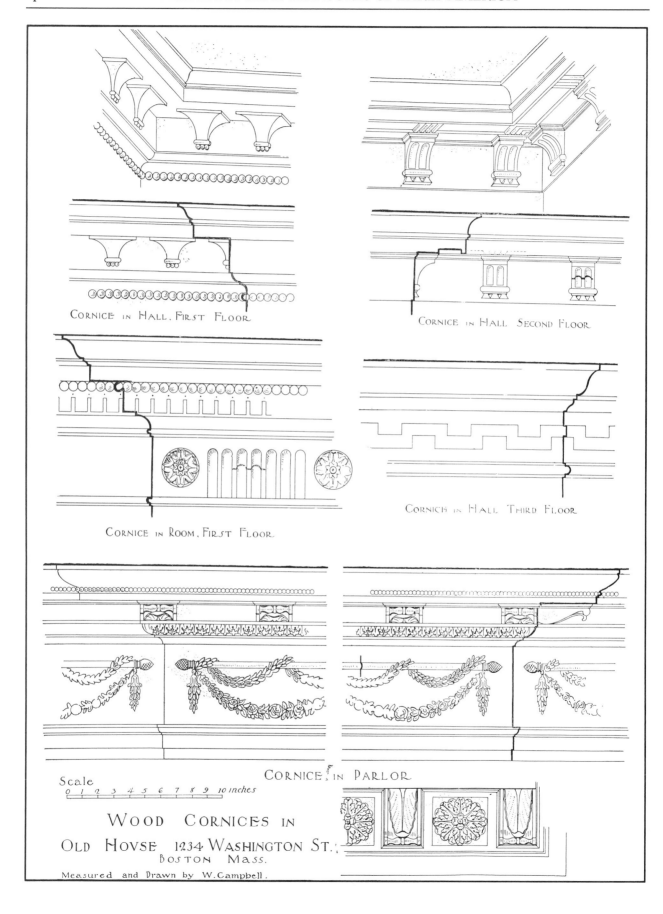

CORNICE in HALL, FIRST FLOOR

CORNICE in HALL SECOND FLOOR

CORNICE in ROOM, FIRST FLOOR

CORNICE in HALL THIRD FLOOR

CORNICE in PARLOR

Scale
0 1 2 3 4 5 6 7 8 9 10 inches

WOOD CORNICES in
OLD HOVSE 1234 WASHINGTON ST.
BOSTON MASS.
Measured and Drawn by W. Campbell.

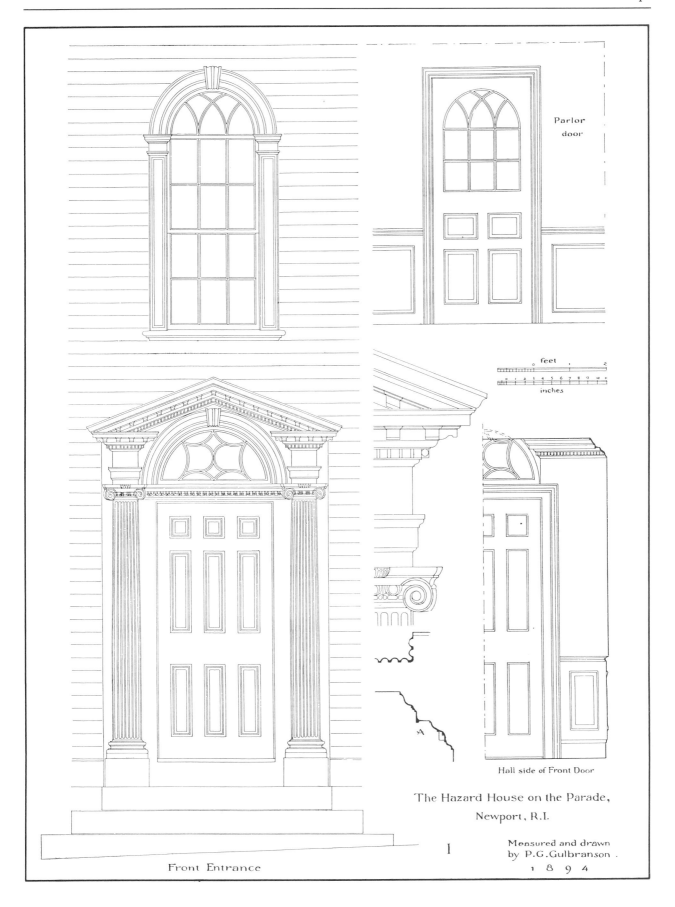

Parlor
door

feet

inches

Hall side of Front Door

The Hazard House on the Parade,
Newport, R.I.

Measured and drawn
by P.G.Gulbranson.
1 8 9 4

Front Entrance

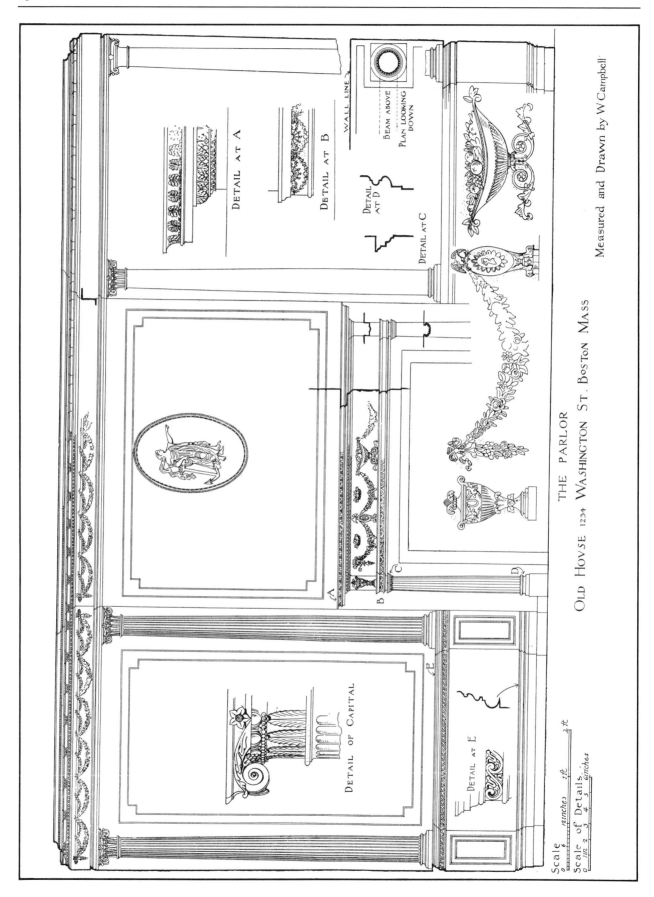

DETAIL AT A

DETAIL AT B

WALL LINE

BEAM ABOVE

PLAN LOOKING DOWN

DETAIL AT D

DETAIL AT C

DETAIL OF CAPITAL

DETAIL AT E

Measured and Drawn by W Campbell

THE PARLOR

OLD HOVSE 1234 WASHINGTON ST . BOSTON MASS

Scale   12inches   1ft   2 ft

Scale of Details   6inches

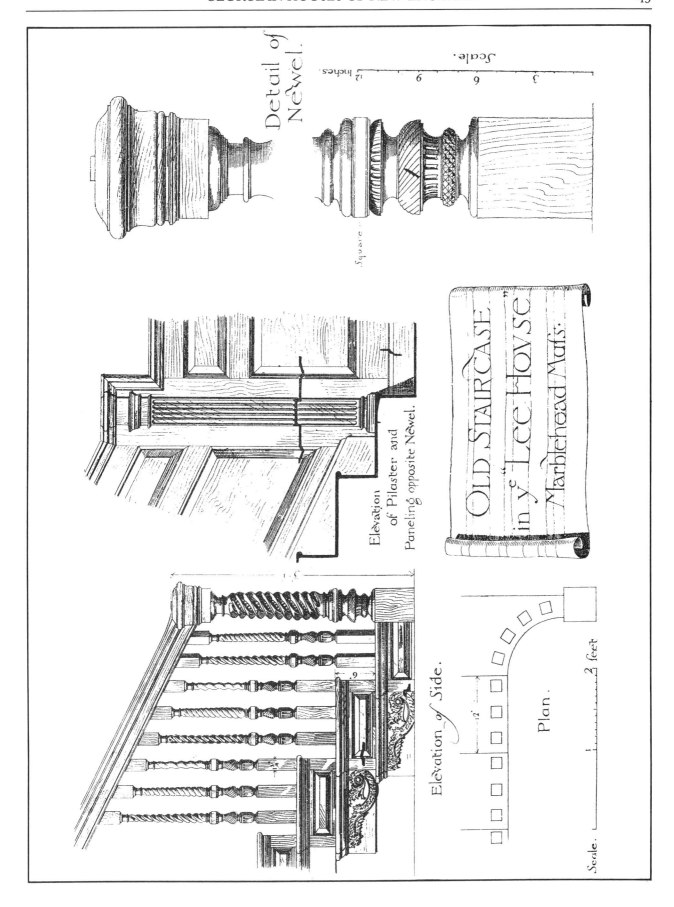

Detail of Newel.

Scale.

Square

Elevation of Pilaster and Paneling opposite Newel.

OLD STAIRCASE in yᵉ Lee Hovse Marblehead Mass:

Elevation of Side.

Plan.

Scale.

Sketches in Providence R.I.

A typical Providence Residence of 50 or 60 yrs ago.

A couple of Residences with Stores under on South Main St: built about 50 years ago.

Yard and Stabling to the above

in the Parlor

Mantelpiece on Second Floor

Door-head in Hall.

Door-head in Parlor.

·The Brown-
·Gammell House·

·Providence·R·I·
·[1786]·

Morning-Room.

Sketches by E.Eldon.Deane.

"The Approach"

The Brown-
Gammell
House·

·Providence· R· I·
·[1786]·

The old : ROYALL MANSION : Medford : Mass :

Court yard Front

Guest Chamber

Garden Front

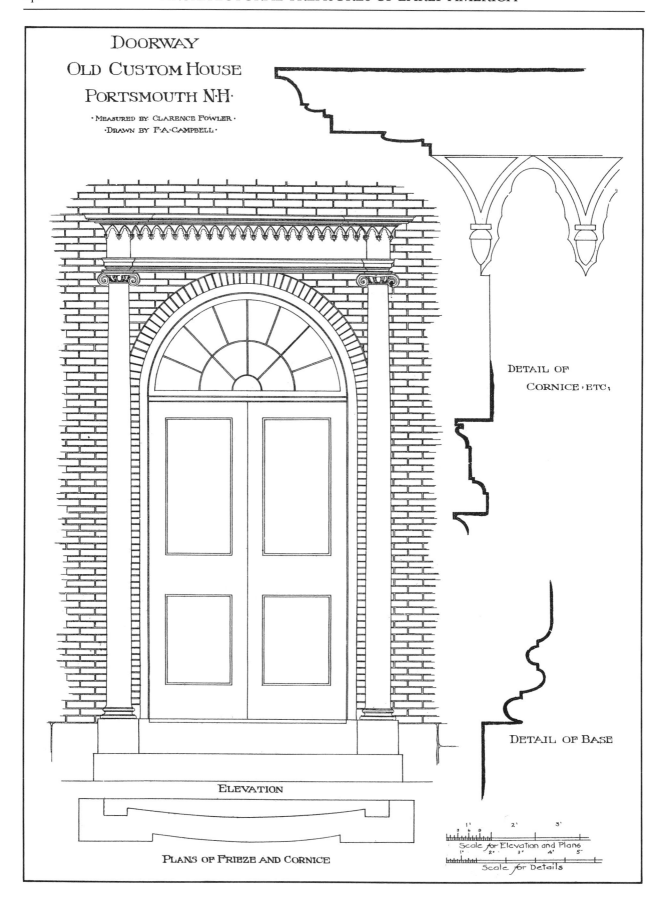

DOORWAY
OLD CUSTOM HOUSE
PORTSMOUTH N·H·
·MEASURED BY· CLARENCE FOWLER·
·DRAWN BY F·A·CAMPBELL·

DETAIL OF
CORNICE·ETC,

DETAIL OF BASE

ELEVATION

PLANS OF FRIEZE AND CORNICE

Scale for Elevation and Plans

Scale for Details

SOUTH ELEVATION

· WEST · ELEVATION ·
ROYAL HOUSE, MEDFORD, MASS.
MEASURED AND DRAWN BY A. C. FERNALD & F. C. ADAMS.

· DETAILS OF EAST ELEVATION ·

· ROYAL HOUSE ·
· MEDFORD MASS ·
· MEASURED BY A·C·FERNALD & F·C·ADAMS ·
· DRAWN BY FERNALD ·

SCALE

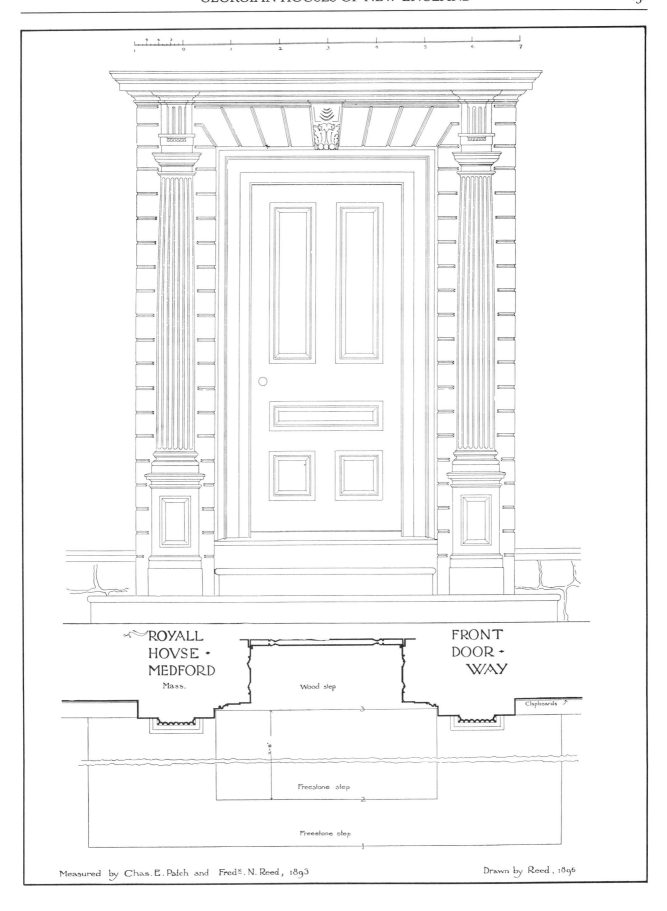

ROYALL
HOVSE ·
MEDFORD
Mass.

FRONT
DOOR ·
WAY

Wood step

Clapboards

Freestone step

Freestone step

Library Door
ISAAC COOK HOUSE—1798—BROOKLINE, MASSACHUSETTS

Mantel
ISAAC COOK HOUSE — 1798 — BROOKLINE, MASSACHUSETTS

WINSLOW HOUSE—1755—PLYMOUTH, MASSACHUSETTS

Porch
JUDGE WALKER HOUSE—1804—LENOX, MASSACHUSETTS

Doorway

BENEFIT STREET, PROVIDENCE, RHODE ISLAND

Doorway

HOUSE AT MANTON, RHODE ISLAND

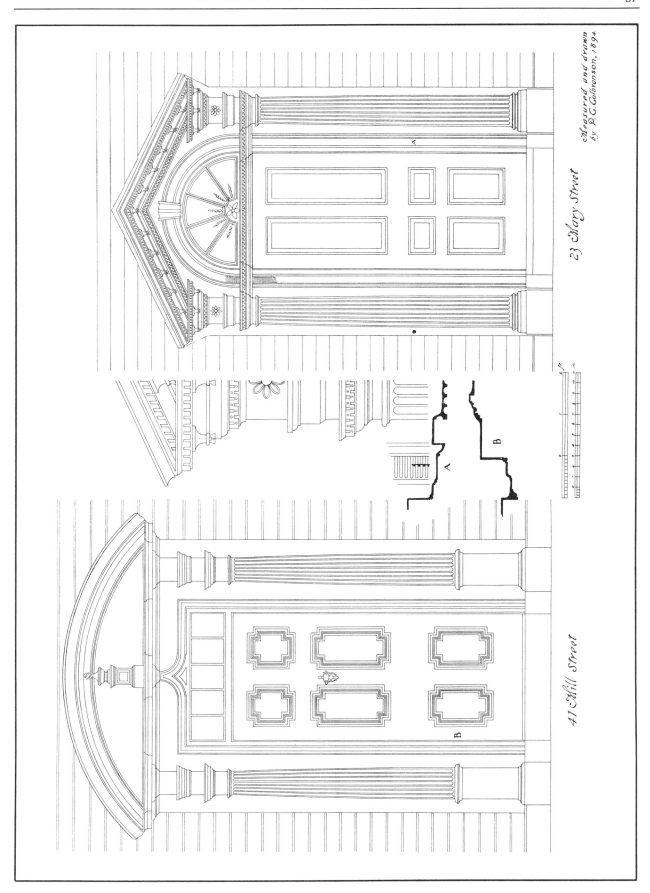

23 Mary Street

Measured and drawn
by P. G. Galbranson, 1894.

41 Mill Street

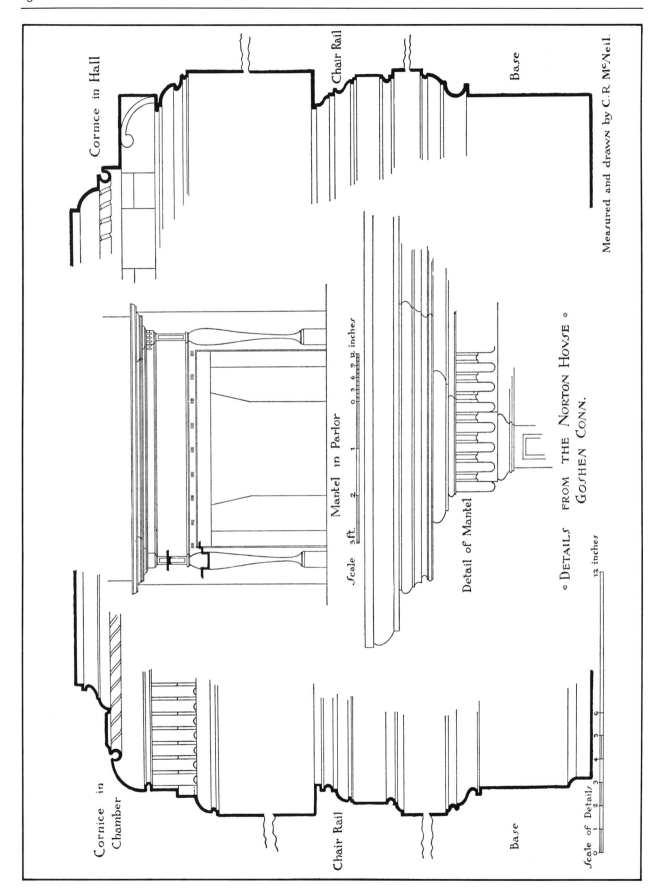

Cornice in Hall

Chair Rail

Base

Measured and drawn by C. R. McNeil.

Mantel in Parlor

Scale 3 ft.

Detail of Mantel

0 3 6 9 12 inches

° DETAILS FROM THE NORTON HOVSE °
GOSHEN CONN.

Cornice in Chamber

Chair Rail

Base

Scale of Details

12 inches

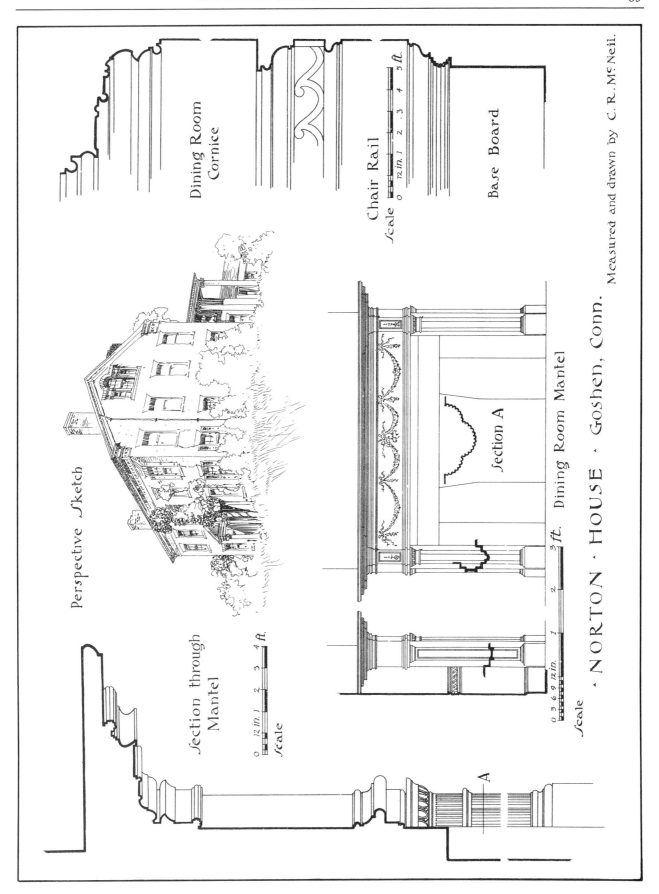

Dining Room Cornice

Chair Rail

Scale 12 in. 1 2 3 4 5 ft.

Base Board

Measured and drawn by C. R. Mc Neil.

Perspective Sketch

Section A

Dining Room Mantel

Section through Mantel

Scale 0 12 in. 1 2 3 4 ft.

Scale 0 3 6 9 12 in. 1 2 3 ft.

A

· NORTON · HOUSE · Goshen, Conn.

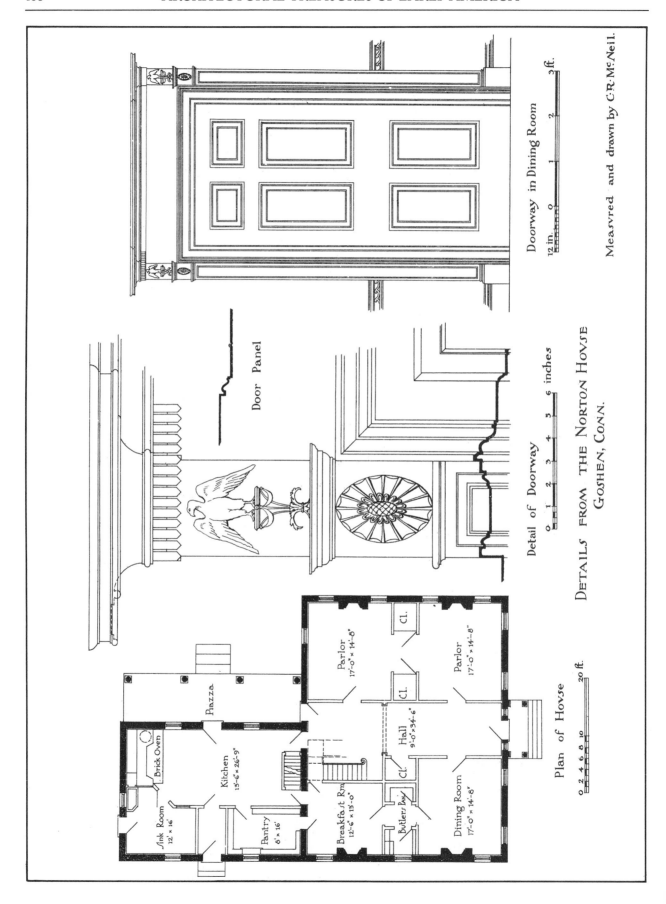

Doorway in Dining Room

12 in. 0 1 2 3 ft.

Measvred and drawn by C. R. McNeil.

Door Panel

Detail of Doorway

0 1 2 3 4 5 6 inches

DETAILS FROM THE NORTON HOVSE
GOSHEN, CONN.

Parlor
17'-0" x 14'-8"

Cl.

Parlor
17'-0" x 14'-8"

Cl.

Hall
9'-0" x 34'-6"

Cl.

Piazza

Brick Oven

Sink Room
12' x 16'

Kitchen
15'-6" x 26'-9"

Pantry
8' x 16'

Breakfast Rm
12'-6" x 13'-0"

Butlers Pry

Dining Room
17'-0" x 14'-8"

Plan of Hovse

0 2 4 6 8 10   20 ft.

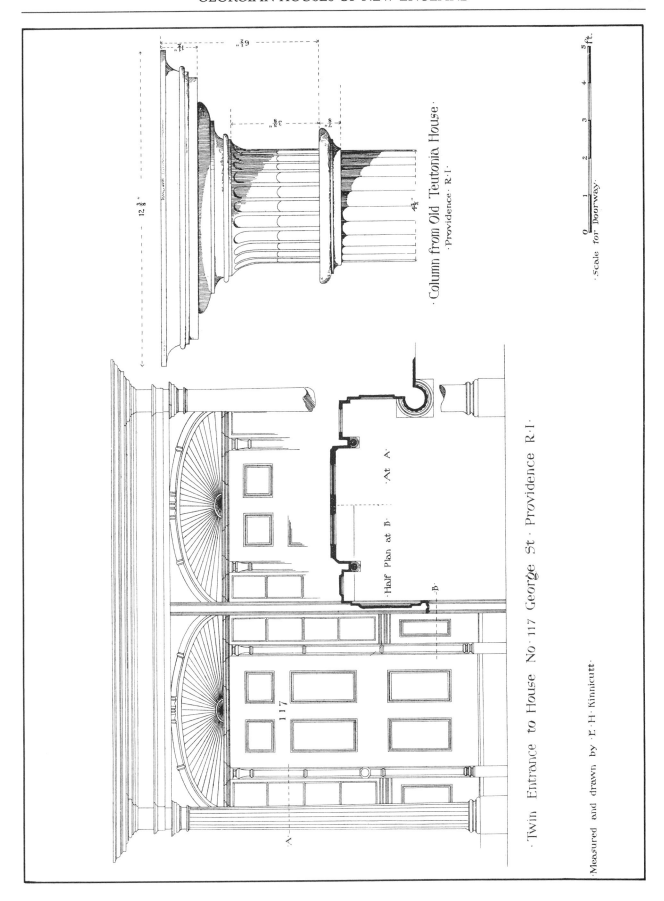

· Column from Old Teutonia House ·
· Providence · R·I·

· Half Plan at B·   · At A·

117

· Twin Entrance to House No· 117 George St· Providence R·I·

· Scale for Doorway·

Measured and drawn by· F·H·Kinnicutt·

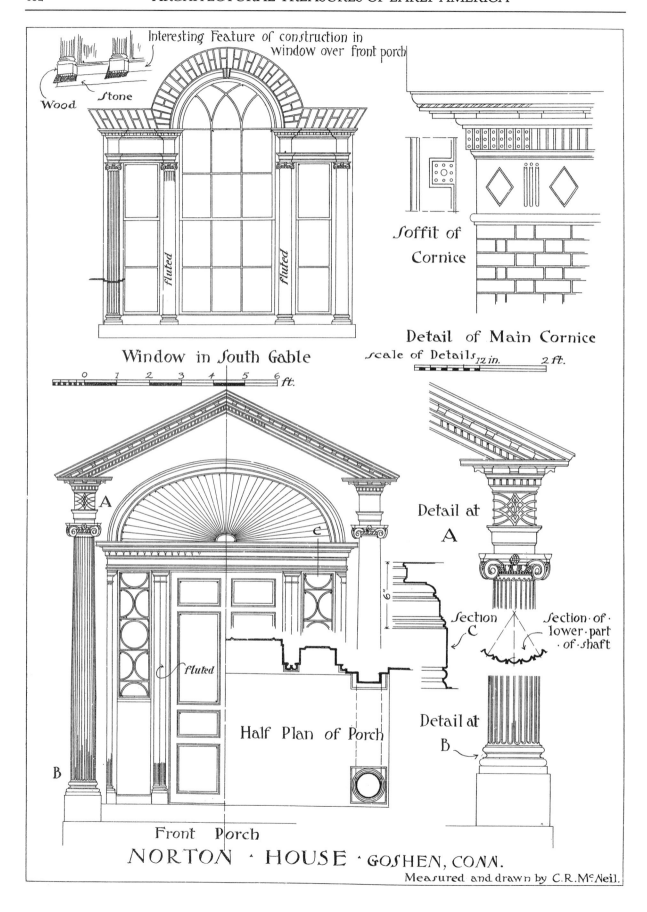

Interesting Feature of construction in window over front porch

Wood   Stone

Window in South Gable

0 1 2 3 4 5 6 ft.

Soffit of Cornice

Detail of Main Cornice

Scale of Details 12 in.   2 ft.

A

fluted

Half Plan of Porch

Detail at A

Section C   Section of lower part of shaft

Detail at B

B

Front Porch

NORTON · HOUSE · GOSHEN, CONN.

Measured and drawn by C. R. McNeil.

Greek Revival and
Some Other Things

Text by
Unknown Author
Originally published in 1902 as
Volume III of The Georgian Period

Side Porch
JONATHAN CHILDS HOUSE — 1800 — ROCHESTER, NEW YORK

THE GREEK REVIVAL AND SOME OTHER THINGS

SOME reviewers of this work have expressed the belief that its title ought to have been "The Georgian Style," and not the, as they maintain, rather misleading title that was actually adopted. If it had been the intention to confine the enquiry to the Free-Classic work commonly known in this country as Old Colonial and in England as Georgian, the name they suggest would have been fitting enough, but, as the enquiry was to have a broader scope, a more comprehensive title was desirable, and the one chosen, covering, as it does, the century or so between the crowning of the first English George and the death of the last one (1714–1827), afforded the latitude that was sought and at the same time indicated that work in the Georgian style was, after all, the chief consideration. Because of this broader title it has been possible to examine not only the vernacular work of the ingenuous early builder, often picturesque and not seldom of much significance, but as well, in some slight way, the work of the Dutch, Swedes, Germans, and to hint that the work of the French and Spanish settlers, which had in it hardly a trace of the influence of the Georgian style proper was, nevertheless, characteristic and interesting.

With more space and time, it would have been interesting to show how distinct an influence on Pennsylvania architecture the building traditions of the Welsh immigrants had had. Wyck, an interesting Colonial building in Germantown, was built for a Welsh owner, and there are others. But the influence of this branch of the Celtic family is shown in the prevailing liking for stone buildings and, particularly,

in the abundant use of dormers and gables with roofs at forty-five degrees, so abundant in modern work in the outskirts of Philadelphia.

The result of this scheme of procedure has been that there has been brought to the attention of the reader the fact that there are several distinct types of buildings existing and still exerting their influence in different parts of the country, types which can hardly withstand much longer the leveling influence of the more easy intercommunication of modern days and the subtle undermining of traditionary methods by the fashion of the hour.

In one particular the unstated programme had to be varied: it was distinctly the purpose to eschew and avoid the buildings erected under the influence of the Greek Revival; but a fuller consideration of the work in the South showed that, if work carried out under the influence of the Greek Revival were to be left out of the examination, a very considerable quantity of interesting buildings, thoroughly typical of the Southern states and forming a very characteristic group in our heterogeneous architecture, would have to go without description and illustration, and to omit these seemed liked introducing at the last moment an unnecessary rigidity into a very elastic programme. For these reasons the work of the post-Georgian period is exhibited with some freedom in these closing pages. Moreover, while the revived interest in Grecian forms seems to have been felt earlier in the South than at the North, it was not, as a cult, honored with the same strict observance that Northern designers yielded. The disease, to call it so, was of rather a mild type, though

A MONUMENT OF THE REVOLUTIONARY PERIOD.
The old Powder Tower. Somerville, Massachusetts

of long persistence, and the result is that, while there are to be found here and there a temple-fronted house such as is found in the North in multitudes, the greater part of the buildings which show the influence of Greek forms show them, not bookishly pure, as in the North, but blended with the Free-Classic of Georgian work and the vernacular of the native builder. The amusing liberties that have been taken with the accepted parts and proportions of the orders which are to be noted in almost any specimen of Southern work are to be attributed partly to the employment of slave labor and partly to that illiteracy of the white mechanic-class in the South which made them less faithful students of such books and drawings as came in their way.

That the Greek movement should have begun earlier in the South—if it did really begin earlier—than in the North is entirely reasonable. The Southern planter traveled abroad more persistently and in greater numbers than did the members of the merchant and manufacturing classes of the Northern

states. Climatic change was more frequently desirable, for one thing, and for another, as the planter class were largely mere spenders of income, the real business of their estates being managed by factors and overseers, they had both the idle time and the accumulated income to spend in travel. In this way they became cognizant of what was the newest fasion in architecture, and, returning home, had their next buildings designed in the new mode—as they remembered it. The Northerner, on the other hand, heard of the Greek Revival mainly by correspondence and obtained his data from imported books, which his skilled mechanics were able to follow accurately and textually, and the buildings that were created through their aid, having the pedantic stiffness that was to be expected, merely emphasized the fact that a Greek temple was never designed to give homelike and appropriate surroundings for English or American men and women of the nineteenth century.

The Southern designers, whether amateur or professional, on the other hand, succeeded in making a

MARITIME EXCHANGE, PHILADELPHIA,
PENNSYLVANIA
William Strickland, Architect

fairly individual and interesting "blend" of Greek and
Free-Classic [Roman] forms, which finally crystallized
into a formula, according to which a large number of
plantation-houses—to which, because of their land-
scape setting and their surroundings, the adjectives
"elegant" and "lordly" are not at all inapplicable—
were built, not only in the first quarter of the last
century, but up to the time when building undertak-
ings of all kinds came to an end with the beginning of
the Civil War.

Who designed these houses is not likely to be
known. Jefferson, of course, had an influence, and so
too did Dr. Thornton and Dr. Kearsley, and it is only
probable that some of the men who sent in designs for
the Capitol at Washington, as McIntire, Dobie, Diamond, Lamphire, Blodgett, Mayo and others, men, so
far as we know, of no great ability, may have been
capable of doing in private work something better
than they suggested for the nation's chief building;
some at least had training and were in some degree
practitioners of architecture. Hoban, at any rate, is
known to have practiced in Charleston before he came
to Washington to do the White House, and it is
known that it was a cause of complaint against some of
the early architects connected with the Capitol that

they spent time in working for private clients that
should have been devoted to the government. It is
doubtful if Bulfinch's influence ever extended farther
South than Baltimore and Washington; but Ithiel
Towne built the state house for North Carolina, and
that would give him an introduction to planters who
were within visiting distance of the state capital; and
we fancy that if Latrobe's[1] drawings should be examined it would be found that he had not a few clients in
the South. McComb, too, a man whose work is less
known than ought to be the case, and who doubtless
built some of the houses along the Hudson, may well
have had Southern clients, and where, later, the Greek
influence is very marked, Strickland,[2] whose Maritime
Exchange in Philadelphia is a striking piece of work,
may well have had a hand in it. But it is not to be
assumed that trained skill was always employed.
Americans are good imitators, and a model to set the
fashion for the local mechanic was all that was needed
for a neighborhood. The variations in the conditions
of the problem and the passion for exercising the native inventive faculties were enough to prevent the
later buildings from being mere textual copies.

The effect of the existence of a type or, it may be,
merely of a pattern, or, again, the mere presence of a
single individual in a neighborhood, is interestingly
shown in the little decayed town of Duxbury, Massachusetts, where in the Waterman House we came
upon a mantelpiece which was not only interesting at
first sight, but seemed to be absolutely unique. Further investigation proved, however, that there were
other houses in the town in whose mantels the novel
treatment of pilaster and frieze was repeated: it was a
common local form, common, perhaps, to other towns
on the Cape, but not found elsewhere.

Stuart and Revett's first book was published, in
parts, between 1762 and 1816, and, as many Southern
gentlemen besides Jefferson left with their book deal-
ers in London and Paris orders to send them with their
yearly or semi-annual supplies any books that were
attracting notice, it is possible that American work was
more or less tinctured with the coming style long before the revival broke upon us with full force. The
architects of the present day are so possessed with the
belief in their own unimpeachable value in and to the

[1] LATROBE, BENJAMIN—Amongst the private houses in
Washington built by Latrobe are the Decatur House, on Lafayette
Square, and the Van Ness House, now a drinking-resort for ne-
groes, at the foot of Seventeenth Street.

[2] STRICKLAND, WILLIAM—Born in Philadelphia, 1787. Studied architecture under Benjamin Latrobe. Died in 1854. His last
work was the state house at Nashville, Tennessee, unfinished at the
time of his death. Besides the Maritime Exchange, in Philadelphia,
in which city most of his work lies, he was the architect of the Mint,
the Naval Asylum and the old Masonic Hall.

HOUSE OF HENRY W. GRADY, ESQ., ATHENS, GEORGIA

world of art that they seem blind to the fact that in this country there were architects before them; that these well-proportioned and delicately detailed mansions, which men and women of feeling now delight in, are the certain evidence of the existence of architects quite as truly artists as any of the architects of today whose income may be ten times as great. The fact that these honored buildings are, generally speaking, the work of nameless men is but a reminder that, for all his braggadocio, the fashionable architect of the hour will himself be unknown to posterity and his name never associated with some possibly good and delicate piece of work of his that may have endured the wear and tear of ages.

The chapter in Volume XV entitled "Georgian Architecture in Dublin" shows some part of the large amount of interesting Georgian work that is to be found in Dublin, and, as it was in Dublin that James

Hoban[3] acquired his training, it is but natural that the work he designed in this country should seem first cousins to that by which his susceptible early years were surrounded. Hoban was one of the first of the many Irishmen who have done much to elevate the intellectual character of this country, just as his more humble countrymen have done much to improve its physical conditions. His name, as long as the White House at Washington stands, will be known to, and remembered by, intelligent enquirers, although it may not have as wide a popular repute as Major L'En-

[3] HOBAN, JAMES — Born in Kilkenny County, Ireland, about 1762. Educated in Dublin. Emigrated to Charleston, South Carolina, in 178–. Designed the state house at Columbia, South Carolina (since burned). Introduced to General Washington by Governor Laurens, of South Carolina. Won the competition for the President's mansion, and afterwards was always in Government employ — as Superintendent of the Capitol, Inspector of Government Work, Surveyor of Public Buildings. He died in 1831.

HOUSE AT BRENTVILLE, PRINCE WILLIAM
COUNTY, VIRGINIA

fant's,[4] who, if his fame had depended on Robert Morris's uncompleted house, instead of upon his plan for the city of Washington, would have hardly had a happier fate than has befallen the designers of some of the admirable work of the eighteenth century.

Equally admirable in their way, in spite of their belonging so pronouncedly to the Greek school and to the nineteenth century, are four houses which may have been designed by the same hand in spite of their being so widely separated as Nashville and Savannah. Perhaps there was a blood-tie between the McAlpins of Savannah and Andrew Jackson, perhaps it is only a case of hero-worship, but, quite as likely, it is a case where inspiration and suggestion originated with the architect. In any case Hermitage,[5] the well-known home of Andrew Jackson, the shrine of many a Democratic pilgrimage, has a namesake in the Hermitage of the McAlpin family, built on the Savannah River, near Savannah, about 1830, and that, in turn, has what might almost be called a repetend in the McAlpin House in Savannah itself, while an even closer likeness is found in the house[6] of James K. Polk at Nashville. (See Volume XIV, Chapter 1.) It is true that the porch

of President Polk's house is distyle in antis, while the Hermitage on the Savannah River has a tetrastyle portico, but the order is the same, and the general air of sober understanding that each structure betrays certainly suggests that one was directly inspired from the other, even if different architects were employed on the two mansions. In both of these houses, and also in the McAlpin city-house, the architect has used the order of the Temple of the Winds at Athens, and at Nashville, where the columns are set in antis, the portico has a somewhat Egyptian air, which is well carried out by the broad wall-spaces about it. It is rather singular that with such good examples—for the capital of the Temple of the Winds is a very graceful one—within reach, and widely known because of the many visitors to General Jackson's house, this order was not more frequently used.

One would think that the general refinement of the Colonial work would have led to an appreciation of the elegance of this particular order, but for some reasons its merits were disregarded and fashion turned in the direction of the more elaborate and far less satisfactory order of the Choragic Monument of Lysicrates, which seems to have been a general favorite. In the Jonathan Childs House, Rochester, New York, we find the capital of this order reproduced with great exactness, while in certain cases in the South we have noted that certain simplifications—not always the same—have been introduced, which seem to show that either the designer felt he was exercising a permissible license or else that the workmen were not as well skilled in following drawings as were the mechanics of the Northern states. The latter is probably the most plausible explanation, for on every side we find little ungrammatical variations which could hardly have been intentional on the part of a competent designer, but are obviously the oversights that an unlettered copyist

---

[4] L'ENFANT—Besides preparing the design for Robert Morris's great house, L'Enfant was the architect of a house in Philadelphia, built for Nicholson, Morris's partner and also Treasurer of the State of Pennsylvania. The Nicholson House, which cost $50,000, has recently been sold for use as a Jewish Orphanage.

[5] THE HERMITAGE, NASHVILLE, TENNESSEE—General Jackson built this house in 1819. It was, however, partially burned in 1835, but was rebuilt in that and the following year. It is now in the charge of the Ladies' Hermitage Association and is essentially a museum of Jacksoniana. General Jackson, who died in the house, was, after the fashion of the day, buried in the front yard.

[6] THE POLK MANSION—This house was not built for, but purchased by, President Polk from the Dickson family, to the descendants of which the property has now reverted. President Polk's tomb, also, stands in the yard.

HOUSE AT BRENTVILLE, PRINCE WILLIAM
COUNTY, VIRGINIA

CHETWOOD HOUSE, EAST JERSEY STREET,
ELIZABETH, NEW JERSEY

or an unskilled mechanic would be guilty of. Thus, we find Roman Doric bases needlessly obtruding themselves beneath a Grecian Doric shaft where no base at all was needed, and, again, a Grecian Doric shaft crowned simply by a square abacus with no echinus below it, this shaft, too, setting upon a square plinth of the same size and thickness as the abacus at the top so that the column might be turned end for end without altering the effect—and it is curious that the effect is really very Grecian, after all. In the case of the Hansell House in Rosewell, Georgia, where the masonry shaft was heavily coated with stucco—quite after the Grecian manner—the mason, in endeavoring to indicate the hypotrachelium, or gorgerin, or whatever is the right name for the incised lines which in the Greek Doric play somewhat the part that the astragal plays in the Roman orders, made a very broad incision all around the shaft with the point of his trowel, but unfortunately held its blade the wrong way, so that the shadow effect is lost and no proper drip is formed.

Even in the case of such a mansion as Arlington, best known now as the home of General Robert E. Lee, but originally built, in 1802, by George Washington Parke Custis, the grandson of Martha Washington, a building designed with much care and intended, so far as the portico goes, to repeat the Temple of Theseus at Athens, we find that the designer did not thoroughly know the style. (See Volume XII, Chapter 3.) It is true that the portico is, like its original's, hexastyle and the ponderous shafts have no bases, but rest properly on a simple stylobate; but it is equally true that the shafts have no cannellations [the dictionaries do not recognize this word, but it is just as

good and useful as the verb "cannelate" that they do admit], and the frieze has been given Roman in place of Grecian triglyphs. It is such little grammatical slips as these that, although they make the purist sniff scornfully, really add to the interest of the Southern work, for it is really only by taking liberties with time-hallowed precept and established practice that changes are made and improvements, possibly, brought about. There is no more propriety for scorning the authors of such vagaries as these than there is reason for condemning them for taking liberties with the proportions of their orders, and recklessly disregarding Vignola's admonitions that a Corinthian column should have only ten diameters for its height. The Southern planter needed verandas, covered ones, and partly for economy's sake and more because it was the fashion of the hour wanted his porticos to protect two stories, but when he found that if he did what Vignola told him to do, the floor-space would be needlessly taken up by huge shafts that really supported no weight at all, and that his house would look more like a temple than a house, he decided to give his columns just such proportions as suited his problem, no matter what the books said. So if, as at Etowah Heights, on the Etowah River, Georgia, the place of the Stovall-Shellman families, we find columns of great attenuation, we feel merely that the practical problem of daily needs has been solved. Here at Etowah Heights another difficulty was overcome, with some success and much ingenuity. It was obvious that it would never do to crown such lofty shafts with a simple Doric capital, the height demanded at least Corinthian treatment; and evidently the working out of a Corinthian cap was beyond the capacity of any of the workmen. But a satisfactory compromise was reached by building a bell, octagonal in plan, out of a series of mouldings

OLD WROUGHT IRONWORK, PROVIDENCE,
RHODE ISLAND

SPROULL HOMESTEAD, NEAR CARTERSVILLE,
GEORGIA

and crowning them all with a square abacus. The result is a capital that at a distance serves well enough as a Corinthian cap, while it is only a near view that brings to light that it is an architectural hybrid, sired by Corinthian, dammed by Perpendicular. It is certainly an ingenious solution and one that serves a capital purpose.

It is such pieces of architectural *naïveté* that make much of the Southern work interesting, but they mark, too, a falling away in delicacy of perception from the work that was done in the eighteenth century along the banks of the Virginia rivers. It is almost certain that one could not find anywhere in Virginia such a florid piece of work as Belle Grove, on the banks of the Mississippi, in Iberville Parish, Louisiana, the home of an obviously wealthy sugar-planter, built, it is said, "shortly after the Revolution." (See Volume XIV Chapter 1.) Anything more unlike what one's preconception of what a suger-planter's house of those days might be expected to look like could hardly be encountered. For, in truth, the typical planter's house of that region, of direct West Indian and, so, Spanish derivation, is to be found in such houses as Home Place, in St. Charles Parish, Louisiana, the home of the Haydel family, and Beauvoir, at Biloxi, Mississippi, long the home of Jefferson Davis, and now transferred to the ownership of the Sons of Confederate Veterans, to be maintained as a home for indigent Confederate soldiers. This type of one-story house is particularly attractive, because it so clearly suggests quiet domesticity, and not the pomp and parade to be looked for in houses whose exteriors declare that they contain abundant guest-chambers and elaborate rooms of ceremony. Yet, that the assurance of a spacious welcome, as it were, may be indicated without sacrificing the promise of domestic comfort is satisfac-

torily proved by such houses as Dunleith, built early in the last century by General Dahlgren, near Natchez, Mississippi. That Dunleith is the legitimate development of the type expressed by Beauvoir is obvious at a glance, and the house, in spite of the presence of the unfortunate dormer windows, added by a later owner, is a very perfect and satisfactory specimen of the home of a wealthy planter in the far South. It is interesting, too, as a "reversion to type," expressing, as it does, a complete revolt against the Greek influence: it comes much nearer achieving the gracility of the real Colonial work than does Montebello, the home of the Shields family, which also stands near Natchez, or Burnside, a Louisiana sugar-planter's house on the banks of the Mississippi, built by a Colonel Preston of South Carolina. These three mansions have about as much dignity, propriety and real architectural character as any one could desire, if one consents to accept the second-story galleries as domestic necessities, and hence, as they satisfy real requirement, that they have sufficient architectural propriety to escape challenge for illiteracy. It is to be noted that the owner of Dunleith seems to have had misgivings on this head, and in place of using the usual wooden balustrade for the upper-gallery railing, has sought not to mar the effect of his colonnades by using light iron railings, painted black so as to be practically invisible from a distance. The floors of such upper galleries do not of constructive necessity cut athwart the columns, for the sake of getting a bearing on them; the floors were carried out to the columns because of the desire to secure more floor-space. The proof of this is to be found in those houses

Veranda
SPROULL HOMESTEAD,
NEAR CARTERSVILLE, GEORGIA

ETOWAH HEIGHTS, ETOWAH RIVER,
GEORGIA

which have the second-story gallery extending to hardly more than half the width of the lower one, the floor being supported by a system of concealed cantilevers, as in the case of the Sproull House, near Cartersville, Georgia, a house which is interesting because of being one of the comparatively small number where the Ionic order is used.

While the West Indian type of house with its flattish hip roof is certainly distinctive of Southern architecture, there is a variation of the normal cottage type, common to all parts of the country, which is also distinctively Southern. In these alliance is made between the rather steep pitched roofs and the supporting columns—of often needless robustness—in so natural a manner that no protest is elicited. A perfect specimen of this class was Concord, before it was destroyed; but there are others built at various dates, but all belonging to the same species. Mrs. Wilson's house, Ashlands, near Mobile, Alabama, is merely one of the class where due regard for the precedents of the type has been observed. Inglehurste, however, built near Macon, Georgia, early in the nineteenth century, shows how the passion for columnar effects has overstepped propriety. Thanks to the luxuriant grace of plants and vines, the fact that these heavy brick piers nowhere support anything but a light wooden roof is

well disguised, and one is aware merely of a delightfully homelike and picturesque effect. This house is absolutely native of the soil; built with timber grown upon and bricks burned upon the place by the labor of slaves, it is because of these things all the more

MEADOW GARDEN,
NEAR AUGUSTA, GEORGIA[7]

[7] Meadow Garden is now preserved by the Walton Memorial Association as a memorial of George Walton, a signer of the Declaration of Independence, who in the older part of the simple structure entertained George Washington in 1791.

FAIRFAX COUNTY COURT HOUSE,
FAIRFAX, VIRGINIA[8]

cherished by its owners and regarded with interest by strangers.

One of the most interesting houses to be found in the South is Edgewood, near Edgefield, South Carolina, interesting because it resumes in itself almost all of the characteristics to which attention has been directed; and the fact that they are shown in this house, once the home of Governor Francis W. Pickens,[9] in a somewhat debased form, seems to indicate that it was recognized that the full expression of the type-form had been reached. Here we have a modest structure, intended for use as an ordinary dwelling, rambling over the ground with true Southern disregard of space till the front spans a length of full forty yards. In the elevation of the first floor above the ground and the absence of rooms at the ground level,

[8] COURT HOUSES—Fairfax County Court House, in Fairfax, Virginia, is a rather typical public building of the pre-Revolutionary period, but it is more interesting because of its association with the Civil War, as it was in the field of military operations, and was at times in the possession of the Federal troops, and, again, in the occupancy of the Confederates. An attempt has recently (c1900) been made to have it transformed into an historical museum, with George Washington's will as its chiefest treasure.

The court house at Chester, Pennsylvania, which was built in 1724, has now a misleading air of quaintness, since the present spirelet-crowned tower, which gives the building its character, is a modern affair and replaces the original belfry.

[9] Governor of South Carolina during the Civil War, 1861–1865. A very pleasant explanation is given for the extreme lateral elongation of this house, an explanation which quite comports with the courteous hospitality of the Southern gentleman. It is said that Governor Pickens could not sleep comfortably if he knew there was a guest sheltering beneath his roof who had been obliged, because of the presence of other guests, to put up with a rear chamber; therefore, he built his house so that all members of the household and all guests must have front rooms—there being no back ones. The story is too pretty to be questioned.

we find a reminder of West Indian derivation, while the division into main house, wing-pavilions and connecting-galleries is distinctly marked. That the architecture is Colonial is told not only by the attempted, and to a good degree successful, refinement of the mouldings of the main portico and the decoration of the front of the raking cornice, but most of all by the artistic feeling that dictated the cutting away of the architrave in a series of elliptical arches. In the flat pediments of the wing-pavilions we find traces of the influence of the Greek Revival, while in the caps and bases of the columns of these pavilions we find the sort of naïve imitations of the proper forms that a colored carpenter might be expected to produce. And then, over and beyond all, the long and roomy veranda is provided as the prime desideratum. The whole structure makes so charming and attractive a composition that one can afford to forget that inaccuracies and imperfections of workmanship exist.

A very satisfactory knowledge of Colonial architecture might be acquired through a study of the older collegiate buildings of the country, more of which are standing than is generally suspected. Besides the "academy" buildings that are still to be found in many New England towns, which, in type, do not vary much from the belfried court houses of the same date, there is a considerable number of dormitories, chapels and halls that were built for the larger institutions of learning that give interesting lessons in proportion and sobriety of decorative treatment. Like her older buildings, Harvard will probably always cherish Bulfinch's University Hall, and Rutgers College, at New Brunswick, New Jersey, will doubtless, in the same way, preserve Queen's Building, designed by John McComb. William and Mary, at Williamsburg, Virginia; St. John's, at Annapolis; the University of Virginia, at Charlottesville, and the University of North Carolina,

South Building Doorway
UNIVERSITY OF NORTH CAROLINA—1798—
CHAPEL HILL, NORTH CAROLINA

HITE HOUSE—1753—WINCHESTER, VIRGINIA

at Chapel Hill, all these and others of the elder colleges have still in use and in good preservation many interesting buildings which are true specimens of Old Colonial architecture, and it would be interesting, sometime, to group them all together.

But, interesting as the later houses are, they are to be regarded rather as marking the transition from the dignified Colonial work to the utterly undignified eclectic work of the present day. If there is any lesson to be drawn from the illustrations in this publication it is that a too free use of applied decorations can be as fatal to a fine piece of architecture as overdressing can be fatal to the asserted gentility of a woman, and many a good design in the Colonial style has in these latter days been made simply tawdry by the mistaken application of moulded decorations in superabundance. Generally speaking, the Northern designer in the eighteenth century showed more reserve, a greater sympathy with the style, a keener appreciation of delicacy than did his Southern brother. To the writer's way of thinking, the much-praised interiors of the Miles Brewton House, in Charleston, are far less satisfactory than many interiors to be found in Salem, Massachusetts, Portsmouth, New Hampshire, and Providence, Rhode Island. Generally speaking, this too lavish use of applied decoration is to be taken as a sign of the decadence, a proof that the building was erected after, rather than before, the Revolution; but that it is not always safe to rely on such an inference is shown by the ceilings at Kenmore, in Fredericksburg, Virginia. (See Volume XII, Chapter 1.) If there ever was a case of over-elaboration this is certainly one, and the observer might well be excused for thinking that the redundancy and repetition, and, above all, the geometrical quality of the general composition, proved satisfactorily that the work and the building were late in date.

But local legend satisfactorily accounts for and excuses this over-elaboration, and the fact that Kenmore, was built by Colonel Fielding Lewis to please his wife, Betty, the only sister of General Washington, tends to prove that it belongs in time with the group of notable Virginia mansions on the James. The story is that these ceilings, overmantels, etc., are the work of certain Hessian prisoners of war who were quartered in the house and probably were delighted to find an agreeable occupation during their enforced idleness, and probably welcomed the money, which was unquestionably paid them, for their labor as a means of providing, possibly, certain delicacies for their mess or warmer clothing for winter wear. Since the mere occupation of idle hours was their chief object, it was natural that the general scheme should be so planned as to consume the greatest number of hours' work, and thus the unneeded quantity is satisfactorily accounted for, while the certain lack of refinement and the geometrical quality of the design may be placed to the credit of the Teutonic understanding of grace.

Kenmore itself has the appearance of being only a part of an uncompleted whole, and considering the standing of the family, it is likely that Colonel Lewis intended to build a more elaborate house than this, and possibly the usual wing-pavilions were to be built later, giving the house finally the general effect of Woodlawn, near Mount Vernon, designed by Dr. Thornton,[10] and for Nelly Custis when she married Lawrence Lewis, the son of Col. Fielding Lewis and Washington's sister, Betty. There is a certain similarity between the two houses, and because of it we may surmise that Kenmore, too, may possibly be one of Dr. Thornton's houses, though it is, of course, possible that Nelly Custis knew all about the house her father had meant to build and so urged Dr. Thornton to make the home of her married life like that which her childhood's home might have been. Otherwise the heavy brick arcade is a meaningless and expensive freak. The arcade itself is unusual, as, with the exception of Mount Vernon, we can recall no other instance of a Colonial house where an arcade is introduced, although it was used in churches and in public build-

---

[10] THORNTON, DR. WILLIAM—Born on the Island of Tortola, West Indies, 1761. Educated in England and, in medicine, Scotland. In 1793 moved to Washington, D.C., and there resided until his death in 1828. He was, in 1794, one of the Commissioners appointed by Washington to survey the District of Columbia, and held the position until it was abolished in 1802. He later became Superintendent of Patents, and held the office up to the time of his death. In addition to his design for the United States Capitol, accepted April 15, 1793, he prepared a design for the President's mansion. In the way of private practice as architect, he designed Montpelier, Orange County, Virginia, for James Madison; the Octagon House, Washington, D.C., for John Tayloe; the Tudor House, Georgetown, D.C., and a few others. (See Volume XII, Chapter 3.)

FEDERAL HILL—1795—
BARDSTOWN, KENTUCKY
The homestead of the Rowan family. The song "My
Old Kentucky Home" was written in this house by
Stephen Collins Foster.

ings, as at Hanover Court House, Fairfax Court House
and others. But in houses the use of the arcade is only
approximated by now and then introducing round
arches in the porches, as at Crewe Hall, Malvern Hill,
Virginia; Gunston Hall, on the Potomac, Mount Airy,
on the Rappahannock, etc. (See Volume XII, Chapters
1 and 3.)

While, as a rule, the eighteenth-century Virginia
mansions were built of brick or wood, some were built
of stone, as, for instance, the Hite House, in Winchester, Virginia, and, the most noted example of all,
Mount Airy, on the Rappahannock, the home of the
Tayloes. Here the portico has an arcade of three
arches, and the galleries connecting the main house
with the wing-pavilions are semicircular in plan, as are
the similar galleries at Mount Vernon. Taken in connection with its setting and its formal garden, Mount

Airy is one of the choicest specimens of Colonial
architecture.

Stone was not infrequently used elsewhere, particularly in Pennsylvania, by the Germans, and in the
Major Duncan House, Paris, Kentucky, we find an
interesting example, first, because it is built of stone
coated with rough-cast, and, next, because its Colonial
character shows how strong a hold the style had on the
people that, at that time, in a new settlement so far
inland as Paris, such a house should have been built.
As might be supposed, its forms and details are based
on reminiscences and so are somewhat simplified and
ungrammatical, as might be expected when neither
designer nor mechanic could drive over to look at the
next house and see "just how the thing ought to be
done." This house and Federal Hill, at Bardstown,
Kentucky, give grounds for believing that the Kentucky towns along the Cumberland Road are deserving
of investigation by whoever next undertakes to con-
sider Colonial architecture.

If one were to trust to inferences and resemblances,
it might be proper to venture the supposition that
there should be included in the list of houses which
were either designed by Jefferson, or whose design was
affected by his advice, the very refined mansion known
as Woodlands that is sometimes miswritten "Geor-
giana" is not unlikely to lead the enquirer into Old
Colonial architecture to think that investigation in
that quarter would be likely to bring to light some
treasure of Free-Classic work. But the place name and
the place itself have nothing to do with the Georges
and their times, and the town has less interest for the
architect than for the historian, for whom it will recall
the story of Plymouth Colony and the attempt of the
Lord Proprietor, Sir Ferdinando Gorges, to establish
for himself a dynastic monarchy in the New World.
Gorges began to send out adventurers in 1606, but not

MAJOR DUNCAN HOUSE—c1790—
PARIS, KENTUCKY

RUFUS GREENE COACH-HOUSE, PROVIDENCE,
RHODE ISLAND

NICHOLS STABLE YARD—1785—
SALEM, MASSACHUSETTS

until 1616 was anything like a settlement established, and that was later abandoned. Gorges was persistent, however, and by 1642 there was enough of a settlement on the Kennebec to make it worth while to secure a city charter for the town of Gorgeana, now York. The town has its architectural interest, however, for here stands, in a good state of preservation, one of the oldest English-derived buildings in the country, the McIntire Garrison (a title which it shares with a few other fortified houses still standing, as at Newburyport, Massachusetts), a two-story house of considerable size, built in 1623, and in which, as also in the old jail now standing and built in 1653, some part of the townsmen found protection at the time of the French and Indian massacre in February, 1692.

That, having before them the thoroughly good and refined buildings that were so common at the close of the eighteenth century, the people of this country should have allowed their buildings of every description to sink to the level of debasing vulgarity that was

reached in the third quarter of the last century is extraordinary, but is far from being unaccountable. The natural love of change for sheer variety's sake had something to do with this abandoning of the safe and well-understood methods; perhaps, even, the impending popular clamor for an "American style" had been heard murmuring in the distance, but neither of these was the most potent cause: this lay in the genius of the race, and there was no escaping from it. The Yankee was created to invent machines, and, giving vent to his passion, before he realized what he had done he had created the "Epoch of the Ready-made." What need was there, then, to think of proportion, or fitness, or propriety, or delicacy, or anything of that sort? All that the human needs of the day could possibly require was to be found in the next shop, and to be bought "by the dozen." Doors, sashes, mantels, newels, cornices, mouldings, there they all were, and all else that was needed was a few nails, a few hours' work, and then you had something vastly better and

MCINTIRE GARRISON — 1623 — YORK, MAINE

more up-to-date than those prim-looking houses the forefathers used to build. The jig-saw is often singled out as the sole cause of this lamentable vulgarization, but, though a large, it was far from being the only offender. The blundering, brutal activity of the machine and the thoughtlessness of the manufacturer, in combination, created the condition which lasted up to the Centennial Exhibition of 1876, at which time it began to dawn on people whose artistic perceptions had not been wholly atrophied that it might be possible to depose the machine from its position as master, and reduce it to its proper sphere as a useful servant; and with the perception of that desirability began the rejuvenescence of arts of all kinds which has been so phenomenal a feature of American progress in civilization in the last quarter century.

It is quite probable that a few years from now, after the lately adopted scheme for the artistic improvement of the city of Washington has developed somewhat, and the parkway between the Capitol and the Memorial Bridge has come to be more used, people will become more familiar than they now are with the south front of the White House and will come to realize that the south front is the front that James Hoban, patterning his plan after the Virginia fashion of fronting the house upon the river highway, intended should impress and welcome the visitor to the dwelling-place of the Nation's ruler. The portico on the north front is of a later time than Hoban's, and as it has a certain satisfactory dignity of its own and is in reasonable accord with Hoban's work, it has for many years successfully dignified the north front and deluded visitors with the idea that they were approaching Hoban's front door instead of actually the rear one. In all probability, the renovations and alterations in and about the White House now just completed will be voted by most people to be satisfactory and successful, and, doubtless, this building now expresses very much what Hoban himself might have done if still in practice today. But there is just a possibility that the White House today is no more like the White House that Hoban had in mind to build than the structure which actually housed the first President was like Leinster House, near Dublin, which is said to have inspired Hoban's design.

As the object of these investigations has been to discover and point out types rather than to make a record, however imperfect, of even a large part of the great number of interesting buildings still extant — but for a large part easily reducible to a few groups when architecturally considered — attention should be directed to the Vanderveer House in Flatbush, Long Island, New York, built in 1798. While its Dutch derivation is strongly marked, it has the rather unusual interest of being a balanced and symmetrical composition, a main building and extensions, or

The Old Jail · York, Maine · 1653 ·

MINOT HOUSE, CONCORD, MASSACHUSETTS

VIEW OF WHITE HOUSE, TREASURY BUILDING
AND CAPITOL, WASHINGTON, D.C.
Before the recent restoration.

wings, upon either side, after a fashion not at all common at the North, where it has been rather the habit to extend always in one direction, until at length the middle-class houses[11] of low cost crystallized into what may be called the telescopic type, each successive addition being smaller than the last, looking as if it were the intention that all should be slid together and sheltered within the main structure overnight. The Bergen Homestead, at Flatbush Avenue and the Albemarle Road, in the same township, is a much older building, and belongs to an earlier phase of the Dutch architecture of New York State. Kingston is another New York town still strongly tinctured with Dutch feeling, but the only house now standing that escaped the fire set by the British in 1777 is the Van Steenbergh House, although the Ten Broeck House, built in 1676, where, later, the New York Senate first assembled, and now

purchased and cared for by the state as an "historical monument," was not much injured by the fire.

It is doubtful if the hurrying New Yorker ever gives to Trinity or St. Paul's churchyards a passing thought, except to feel irritation at the idea that any people can be so little worldly wise as not to take steps to get handsome incomes from such costly building sites. Strangers, having more leisure to investigate, know that in both these resting-places there are some interesting tombs and gravestones. Northern churchyards, however, do not show in tombs and gravestones the same architectural qualities that examples of Southern mortuary art offer. The plain slate slab that accords so soothingly with the greens and grays of the country churchyard is rather the type at the North, and while the lettering is often of great elegance, the death's head or cherub's head, with palm branches or wings and a border of conventional leafage, that in varying forms are used as decorations are interesting more because they are archaic than because they are artistic. A large part of their interesting qualities lies in their curious, amusing and often amazing epitaphs. In the latter class is found to be *facile princeps* one in the Phipps Street Cemetery in Charlestown, Massachusetts, which declares that:

HERE LYES INTERRED YE BODY OF

---

[11] MIDDLE-CLASS HOUSES — A very excellent example of the dwelling-house which men of the well-to-do yeoman class built for themselves is the Josiah Day House in West Springfield, Massachusetts, built in 1754, and it may be taken to indicate either a certain change in the building-fashions of the time or else may mark the increasing prosperity of the family, for, whereas this house at West Springfield is substantially built of brick, the Ambrose Day House, built in 1725 by a member of the same family, at Westfield, not far away, was a frame house with a pargeted, or rough-cast, front, a style of exterior finish at one time much in vogue in certain parts of New England.

MRS. ELIZABETH PHILLIPS WIFE
TO MR. ELEAZER PHILLIPS WHO
WAS BORN IN WESTMINSTER IN GREAT
BRITAIN AND COMMISSIONED BY JOHN
LORD BISHOP OF LONDON IN YE YEAR
1718 TO YE OFFICE OF A MIDWIFE AND CAME
TO THIS COUNTRY IN YE YEAR 1719 AND BY
YE BLESSING OF GOD HAS BROUGHT INTO
THIS WORLD ABOVE 130,000 CHILDREN.
DIED MAY 6, 1761. AGED 76 YEARS.

The stone now actually bears this extraordinary record; but the character of the figures and their spacing make it plain that the number of births was three thousand and that it was later maliciously magnified by the prefixing of a one and the suffixing of a final naught.

In the South, where the pomp and circumstance of family were more obvious in daily life, it is natural that the tombs and gravestones should take on a more architecturally monumental air, and many interesting tombs and monuments of the period are to be found in the churchyards and private burying-grounds from Maryland southward, while mural tablets bearing the family coat-of-arms and more or less elaborately treated with carving decorate the church and chapel walls and by the quaint phrasing of their epitaphs make plain that they belong to an earlier civilization than ours.

It must be evident that it was the writer's intention to let this paper end with this slight reference to the last resting-place of the men whose homes in life have been the subject of these investigations, but at the last moment—long after the eleventh hour has struck—

there come to hand photographs of an extremely interesting house at Binghamton, New York, which should not be omitted from a record that has been allowed to extend over into the Greek Revival period. It would be difficult to find a clearer case of Transition—it is pleasant to treat the subject with full architectural dignity—than this little house affords. The original house, with its central hallway, its four chimneys in the outside walls declaring an open fireplace for each of its four rooms and, above all, its porches, both front and rear, is clearly of the eighteenth-century type common to central New York, the front porch showing an interesting vagary in the planning which evidences thought and architectural purpose on the part of the designer. Later, when the Greek movement was the talk of the day, the owner seems to have felt that he must be in the fashion and so built at one end a screen wall with Classic attributes and, to show his originality, quite as much, possibly, as to gain space, introduced a species of two-story bow-window in the middle—essentially repeating the Boston "swell front." The plebeian extensions and additions at the other end of house, added at a still later day, serve to show to what depths of architectural ignorance building matters had been allowed to sink in the third quarter of the last century.

The appearance of this circular or segmental bay or pavilion is something altogether notable, not only as a confirmation of the belief in the swell-front as peculiarly a Boston institution, but also as a reminder of the absence of anything but quadrilateral forms in Southern work, excepting, of course, the fully circular forms adopted for certain outbuildings, as mills, smoke-houses and so on. Even the half-octagonal seems to have been rarely used, the Harwood House in Annapolis being the only building we can recall that exhibits this form, but of a later day we find in the Cobb House near Athens, Georgia, a rather interesting application of the octagonal treatment which also may be considered one of the final forms of development of the wing-pavilion.

GRAVESTONES AT FORT GRISWOLD,
GROTON HEIGHTS, CONNECTICUT

OLDEST STONE COPP'S HILL
BURYING GROUND

GRAVESTONE OF THOMAS CLARK,
MATE OF THE MAYFLOWER,
PLYMOUTH, MASSACHUSETTS

HOUSE OF GEN. T. R. R. COBB,
NEAR ATHENS, GEORGIA

Stable

WOODLANDS—1770—PHILADELPHIA, PENNSYLVANIA

Rear View

WOODLANDS — 1770 — PHILADELPHIA, PENNSYLVANIA

Doorway
WOODLANDS — 1770 — PHILADELPHIA, PENNSYLVANIA
House of William Hamilton

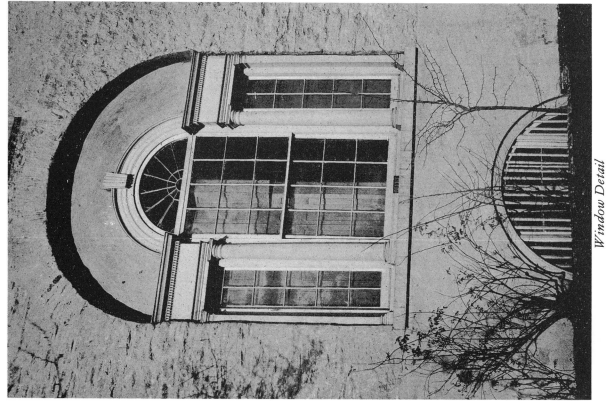

Window Detail
WOODLANDS — 1770 — PHILADELPHIA, PENNSYLVANIA

Front View

WOODLANDS — 1770 — PHILADELPHIA, PENNSYLVANIA

EDGEWOOD, NEAR EDGEFIELD, SOUTH CAROLINA

INGLEHURST, NEAR MACON, GEORGIA

GREENWOOD, NEAR THOMASVILLE, GEORGIA

BEAUVOIR, BILOXI, MISSISSIPPI

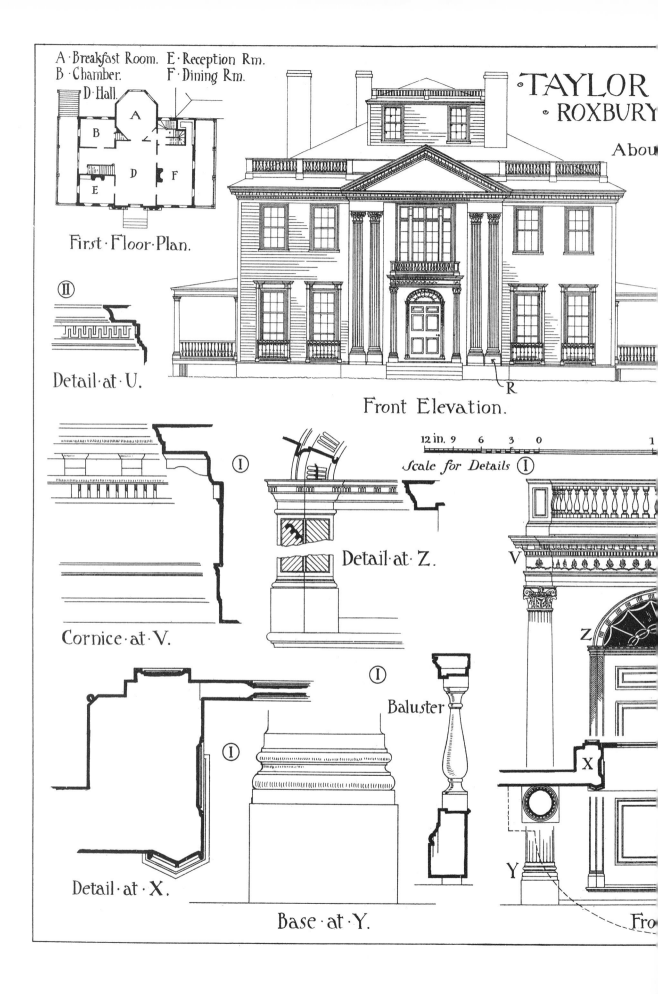

A·Breakfast Room.   E·Reception Rm.
B·Chamber.   F·Dining Rm.
   D·Hall.

First·Floor·Plan.

Detail·at·U.

Front Elevation.

Cornice·at·V.

Detail·at·Z.

12 in. 9   6   3   0   1

Scale for Details

Detail·at·X.

Baluster

Base·at·Y.

TAYLOR
ROXBURY

Abou

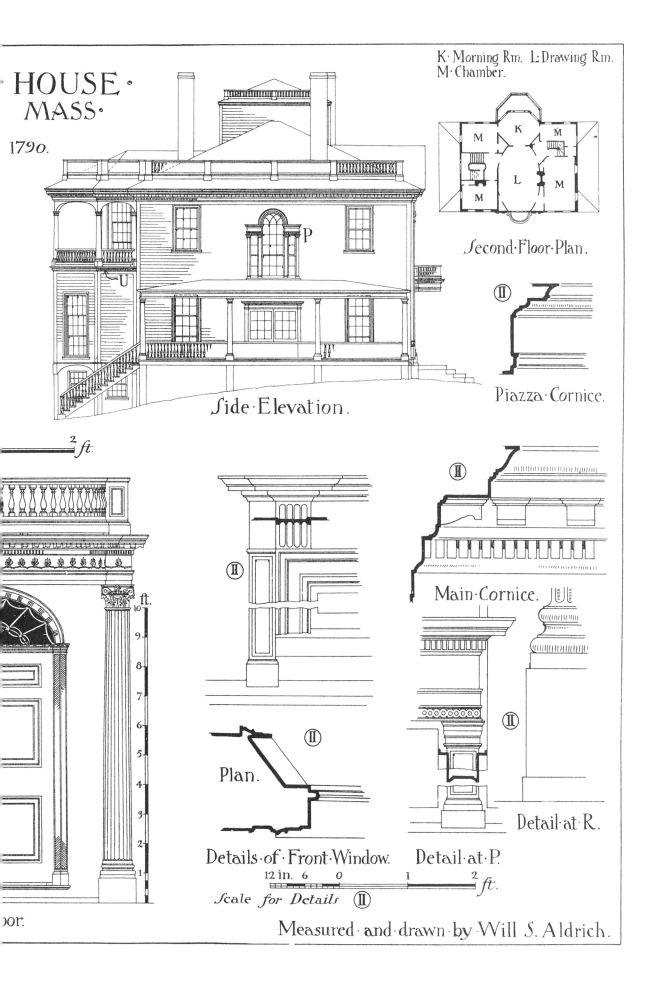

HOUSE·
MASS·

1790.

K· Morning Rm.   L· Drawing Rm.
M· Chamber.

Second·Floor·Plan.

Side·Elevation.

Piazza·Cornice.

Main·Cornice.

Detail·at·R.

Plan.

Details·of·Front·Window.   Detail·at·P.

12 in. 6   0   1   2 ·ft.
Scale for Details Ⅱ

Measured·and·drawn·by·Will S. Aldrich.

A TUSKAGEE, ALABAMA, HOMESTEAD

BURNSIDE, ON THE MISSISSIPPI RIVER, LOUISIANA

First Church
New Haven, Conn.

Old North Church
New Haven, Conn. 1815.

Sketched by G.C.Gardner.

Detail at
A

Section at A

Detail at B

Base of Column

Front Entrance
·NORTH·CHURCH·
·NEW·HAVEN,CONN.

Scale of Details   1   2 ft.

Scale 0   1   2   3   4   5 ft.

Measured and drawn by C.B.French.

HOME PLACE, PARISH OF ST. CHARLES, LOUISIANA
The Homestead of the Haydels

OLD MARMILLION MANSION, PARISH OF ST. JOHN THE BAPTIST, LOUISIANA

South Front
THE WHITE HOUSE, WASHINGTON, D.C.
James Hoban, Architect

Northeast View
THE WHITE HOUSE, WASHINGTON, D.C.
James Hoban, Architect

Front

ASHLANDS, NEAR MOBILE, ALABAMA

ASHLANDS, NEAR MOBILE, ALABAMA

Home of Mrs. Augusta Evans Wilson

MONMOUTH, NEAR NATCHEZ, MISSISSIPPI

DUNLEITH, NEAR NATCHEZ, MISSISSIPPI

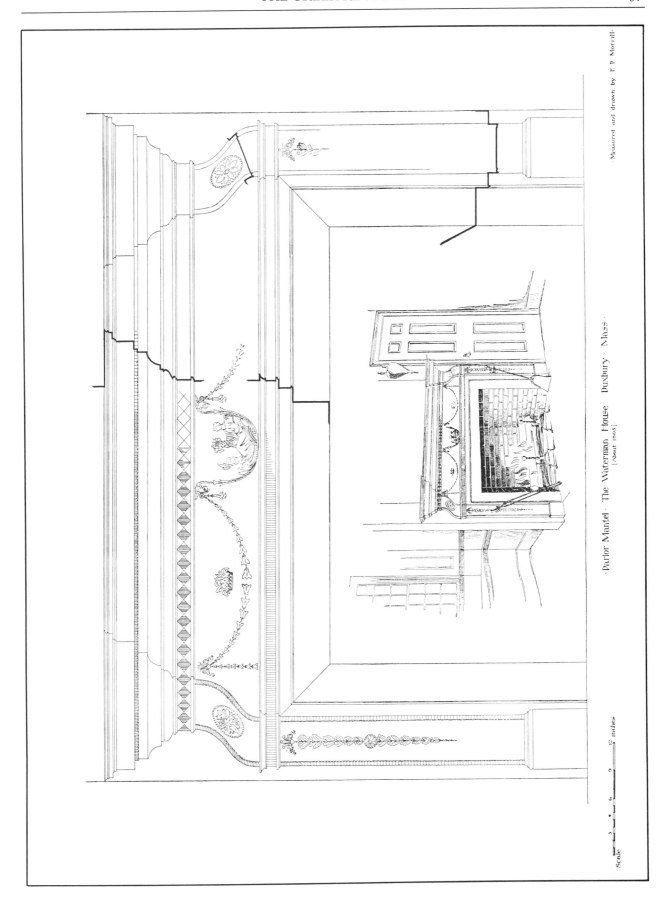

· Parlor Mantel · The Waterman House · Duxbury · Mass ·

·[About 1803]·

·Measured and drawn by E. P. Morrill·

Scale 3 6 9 12 inches

" Edgewood " · near · Edgefield · S · C ·

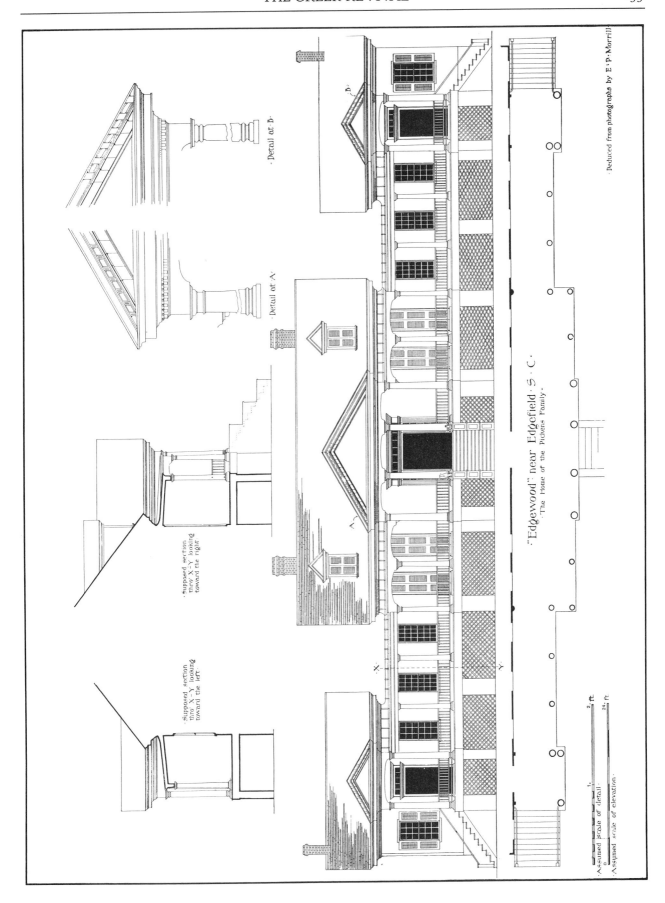

- Detail at B·

- Detail at A·

- Supposed section thro' X–Y looking toward the right·

- Supposed section thro' X–Y looking toward the left·

·"Edgewood"· near Edgefield· S · C ·
·"The Home of the Pickens Family"·

·Deduced from photographs by E · P · Morrill·

2· ft·
·Assumed scale of detail·
0   24· ft·
·Assumed scale of elevation·

Detail of Cornice
JONATHAN CHILDS HOUSE — 1800 — ROCHESTER, NEW YORK

Seventh-Day Baptist Church
Newport, Rhode Island

Text by
George C. Mason, Jr.
Originally published in 1899 as
Volume I of The Georgian Period

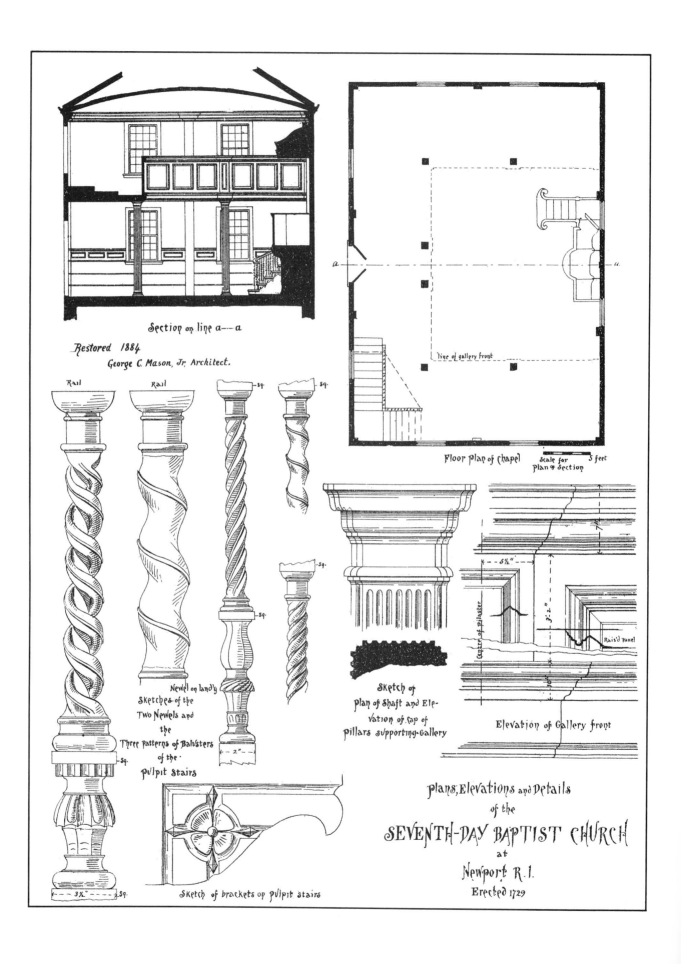

Section on line a—a

Restored 1884
George C. Mason, Jr. Architect.

Rail

Rail

Newel on land'g

Sketches of the
Two Newels and
the
Three patterns of Balusters
of the
Pulpit stairs

Sketch of brackets on pulpit stairs

Floor plan of Chapel

Line of gallery front

Scale for
plan & section

5 feet

Sketch of
Plan of Shaft and Ele-
vation of Cap of
Pillars supporting Gallery

Elevation of Gallery front

Raisd panel

Center of pilaster

Plans, Elevations and Details
of the
SEVENTH-DAY BAPTIST CHURCH
at
Newport R.I.
Erected 1729

THE SEVENTH-DAY BAPTIST CHURCH AT NEWPORT, RHODE ISLAND

THIS venerable edifice, for many years the place of worship of the Seventh-Day Baptist Society in Newport, some years ago passed by purchase into the hands of the Newport Historical Society, and is now occupied by that body as its cabinet and meeting-room. After long disuse, the building was re-opened to the public, with appropriate ceremonies, on the evening of November 10, 1884.

The church, when purchased by the Historical Society was found to be rapidly falling to decay, through long neglect and the action of the elements. A most thorough restoration became necessary, in the course of which portions of the work were entirely replaced with new, the character and ancient detail being scrupulously adhered to.

The Seventh-Day Baptist meeting house, or church, as it is more generally styled, has a history of over one hundred and fifty years, having been erected in 1729. It demands more than a passing notice from the student of Colonial architecture for its venerable and sacred associations. Its structural and decorative features are thoroughly in unison with the best building practice of the second period of Colonial architecture, and are shown in detail in the accompanying sketches made in the church itself, previous to its restoration.

In the year 1678, Samuel Hubbard, one of the seven founders of the Sabbatarian Society in Newport, wrote to a friend in Jamaica, saying, "Our numbers here are twenty; at Westerly, seven; and at New London, ten." From the diary of the same Samuel Hubbard we learn that the church was organized in 1671. The Society always claimed to be the oldest Sabbatarian and the fifth Baptist church in America. The first pastor was William Hiscox, who died May 24, 1704, in the sixty-sixth year of his age. Joseph Maxon was chosen to fill the office of traveling preacher for Westerly in Septem-

ber, 1732, and in October of the same year he was made pastor of both the Newport and Westerly churches. The Newport church, previous to the Revolution, maintained a strong and stirring organization; among its members were men reputable for their talents, learning and ability, and holding honored stations in public affairs. The war scattered the congregation, and the church never recovered its former prestige. Henry Burdick was ordained pastor, December 10, 1807. In 1808 the membership was reduced to ninety, and in 1809 to eighty-seven. The last pastor was Lucius Crandall. The records of the church terminate in 1839, and the last sacred services were held in that year. The sole surviving member of the Society living when the church passed out of the hands of the Sabbatarian trustees was Mrs. Mary Green Alger, who died on the 11th of October, 1884, at the age of ninety-three years, nine months and nine days, just one month previous to the dedication by the Historical Society. The church in the town of Westerly grew and prospered, and is still in a flourishing condition. Under the liberal Charter and Constitution of Rhode Island, the towns of Westerly and Hopkinton have always recognized as holy the seventh instead of the first day of the week. It is a curious sensation to walk through the streets of those towns on a Sunday morning and hear the buzz of machinery and the various sounds of a striving and busy community.

In 1706 the Sabbatarian Society purchased, in the then town of Newport, a lot of land, situated at the junction of what are now known as Spring and Barney streets, from Jonathan Barney, for "twenty-one pounds, six shillings, and eight pence, current passable money at eight shillings per ounce silver." The deed was taken in the name of Arnold Collins, goldsmith, a member of the Society and the father of

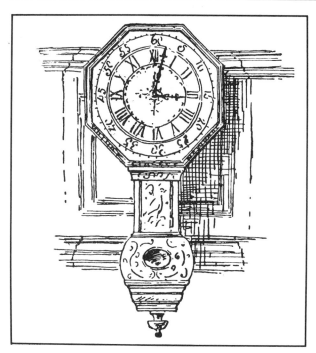

Detail of Clock
SEVENTH-DAY BAPTIST CHURCH,
NEWPORT, RHODE ISLAND

Henry Collins, a distinguished citizen who took an active part in the affairs of the town and colony, and was one of the founders of the Redwood Library, giving the land on which that building stands. Two smaller portions of land were afterwards added to the church lot.

At a meeting of the Society held November 9, 1729, it was voted "that a meeting-house be built, thirty-six feet in length and twenty-six feet in breadth, on part of that land whereon the present meeting house now stands; and voted at the same time that Jonathan Weeden and Henry Collins be appointed a committee to undertake the whole affair of erecting said house, and to raise money by subscription. Voted at the same time that the two afore-mentioned brethren do their endeavors to make sale of their present meeting house to the best advantage they can, and dispose of the money towards the better furnishing of the house they are to erect."

The character of the first meeting house is unknown, but it must have been a very simple affair. The house of 1729 is the subject of this sketch. Like most of the Colonial buildings which I have measured, the dimensions overrun the established plan and instructions. The church measured thirty-seven feet front and twenty-seven feet deep, and all its parts and details are laid out with scrupulous exactitude with reference to symmetry and proportion.

The exterior of the church is of the most severe and barnlike character; with two rows of windows having plank frames, and with a shallow cornice, made up of a gutter and bed-mould, the latter mitreing around the heads of gallery windowframes. The entrance door has no features worthy of notice, and the steps are of Connecticut brownstone, the usual material used for that purpose in Colonial work.

The roof is a simple double pitch, the frame being of oak timber and shown on the sectional drawing. The tie-beams, hewn into curves, are curious instances of framing. All furring-down for the ceiling is dispensed with, and the lathing is nailed directly on the 4" x 4" furrings, which are tenoned between the tie-beams.

All the timbers, with the exception of the tie-beams, are squared. The framing at the junction of the principals and tie-beams was badly conceived, and the hidden tenons rotted off, permitting the building to spread badly. In restoration it became necessary to insert two tension-rods and draw in the walls to their original vertical position. These rods run across the building at the line of the cornice.

The large drawings indicate the conscientious attention to detail which the colonial mechanics were wont to bestow upon their works. The greater part of the inside finish is made of red cedar, painted white. All the members were wrought by hand, and the amount of curved and moulded work, including mitres, is extreme.

While engaged in making the measurements preparatory to the restoration, I was struck by a coincidence which gradually developed as the work progressed. It has always been a mystery, unsolved by investigation, as to who designed Trinity Church in Newport. It was erected in the years 1724–1725, through the instrumentality of the English Society for the Propagation of the Gospel in Foreign Parts. The plans and instructions must have come from England, as it was not until some years later that architects of talent, like Peter Harrison, emigrated to the colonies. It is a free copy of Wren's church of St. James, Piccadilly, having the general character of that edifice, with, however, some strongly marked differences. Instead of the row of Corinthian columns along the gallery, and supporting the vaulted ceiling, it has square and fluted piers, and the lower piers are much smaller, although paneled in the same way as those at St. James's. The ceiling is also different, substituting for a simple barrel-vault an elliptical and groined system of vaulting.

Whoever may have been its architect, the men who built Trinity Church, in 1724–1725, also built the Sabbatarian Church, in 1729. It is not probable that an architect was employed for the latter edifice, but the section of every moulding and detail is the same in both structures, indicating the use of one set of hollow

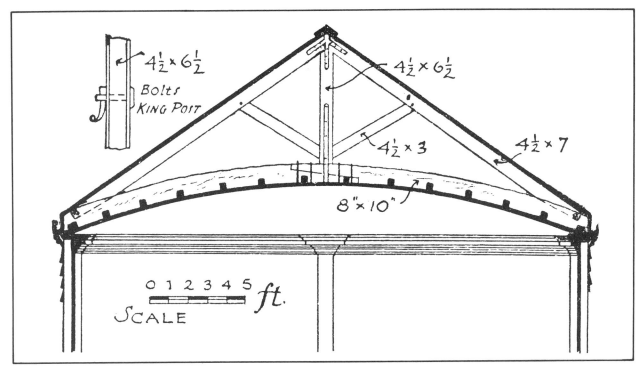

Detail of Roof
SEVENTH-DAY BAPTIST CHURCH,
NEWPORT, RHODE ISLAND[1]

and round planes by the same hands. The designs of the galleries, piers and paneling are also the same. One feature in the Sabbatarian Church is, however, unique; *i.e.,* the pulpit stairs. These stairs, although partaking of all the characteristic features of the best domestic work of the day, are richer in detail and are more delicately wrought than in any other staircase of the time with which I am familiar. The staircase in Trinity Church is of a much simpler design, and the one in the Christopher G. Champlin House, the best domestic example in Newport, shows much less elaboration.

The paneling under the sounding-board of the Sabbatarian Church is the same as that on the ceiling over the warden's pew in Trinity Church, and the small pedestal on the sounding-board was surmounted by an English crown, probably of the same character as the one still remaining on the organ of old Trinity.

The tablets on the wall back of the pulpit, and shown on drawing, were presented to the Society by Deacon John Tanner, in 1773. The lettering is still clear and bright, with scrolls in the arched tops. Below the Decalogue appears the following text from *Romans* III, xxi: "Do we then make void the law through faith? God forbid; yea, we establish the law."

There is a legend that when the English army took possession of Newport, in 1777, and desecrated all the places of worship, except Old Trinity and the Sabbatarian Church, by using them for riding schools and hospitals, the latter edifice was saved and guarded through respect for the Decalogue and the royal crown found within its walls.

The clock, forming the initial cut of this chapter, hangs on the face of the gallery, between the two central piers, facing the pulpit. It was made by William Claggett, a celebrated horologist of his day in Newport. The clock in the tower of Trinity Church was also made by him, and many of the tall clocks, with sun, moon, stars and signs of the zodiac, frequently found in the possession of old families, bear his name. The church clock has been repaired and is again marking the hours, not of long and prosy sermons dealing with colonial brimstone, which seems to have been a very prominent article in the faith of our ancestors, but striking hour after hour the onward march of Newport's history, down from the eventful and romantic past, into the unknown future.

---

[1] The tie-beams are of rough-hewn timber, curved by the axe, scarfed in center. The iron straps are roughly forged and the bolts which secure them to the king-post are simply driven through, the ends turned over and keyed. The timber is all of oak. The furrings for ceiling are about 4" x 4" and tenoned into the tie-beams at each end. The lathing is directly on the furrings. Each principal runs down to a feather end, but is tenoned into the tie-beam and pinned. The building spread badly, and in its restoration iron tension-rods were put in between the plates.

Sketch plan of end of bottom step

Base
Mouldings
of
Pilasters
on
Front of Pulpit

Cap Moulding of Pulpit

Plan of Under side of sounding board

1   2 feet

Elevation
of
PULPIT in SEVENTH-DAY BAPTIST CHURCH,
Newport, R. I.

Erected 1729.

1   2 feet

Restored 1884.

George C. Mason Jr, Architect.

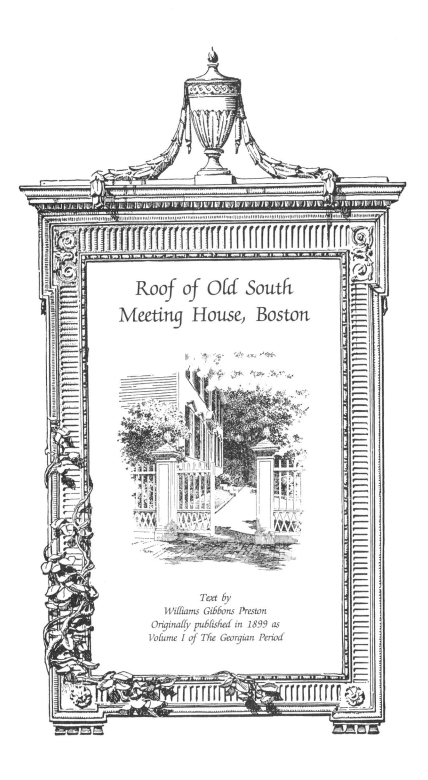

Roof of Old South Meeting House, Boston

Text by
Williams Gibbons Preston
Originally published in 1899 as
Volume I of The Georgian Period

OLD SOUTH CHURCH ✠ BOSTON, MASS.

L.S. IPSEN DEL.

THE ROOF OF THE OLD SOUTH MEETING HOUSE, BOSTON

AS an example of American carpentry of one hundred and fifty years ago, the roof of the "Old South" in Boston merits a passing notice. Having had recent occasion [1876] to examine the building, the accompanying drawing of the roof was made; and as a matter of record, as being a curious example of early colonial work which would be generally interesting, and as an example to others to detail any quaint bit of work falling within their observation, I herewith register a few facts in regard to it.

The roof of the building (which is some 65′ x 95′) is supported by six trusses spaced at about equal distances from each other, but the last truss somewhat farther from the rear wall, in order to avoid too steep a pitch from it to that wall. The workmanship is quite primitive and rude, most of the timber being hewn sticks; and the sapwood at the angles is in many instances affected by dry-rot, or, in common parlance, is "powder-posted."

The trusses are much sprung and distorted, both horizontally and laterally — variously in different trusses; but, from a consideration of some defects common to them all, their story may be guessed with a considerable degree of accuracy. The execution of the roof indicates ship-builders' work; and, in the days when the division of labor had not reached its present development, it is more than probable that men who had served their seven years in the yards of the "Old Country" had a hand in the work. The first step in the construction, which occurred to the builders, was evidently a pair of rafters A A, a tie-beam B, and a king-post C, to support the center of the tie-beam at its point of splicing.

The tie-beam, by the way, is cambered about two and a half feet, nearly following the line of the plastered ceiling hung to it below. Had the tie-beam and ceiling been built level in the first instance, they would evidently have later shared the misfortunes of the principals, and have now been convex instead of concave. Having proceeded thus far in the design for their roof, they next bethought them that the rafters A A, some forty feet in length, without intermediate support, would not be sufficiently stiff to carry the roofing. Now, instead of proceeding to erect struts from the foot of the king-post C, to the principals A A, at about right angles to the latter, and from their points of contact to drop tension-pieces to the tie-beam, and from their feet to erect other struts similar to the first — thus forming a perfectly rigid frame, and obtaining intermediate points of support for each rafter — they let loose the incipient Yankee ingenuity which the east winds were even then infusing into their minds, and, following the bent of a ship-builder's mind, took another course.

They procured stout hewn oak beams, D D, and by some means best known to themselves — either by the coaxing of steaming, or the coercion of pulleys and tackle — formed of them arches; their feet stepped into the tie-beam near the walls, and the other ends keyed in position by wedges passed through a mortise in the king-post. Now they had constructed, within their truss, a sort of bowstring girder, upon which they founded their hopes of supporting the principals A A by means of the blocking, or struts, E E.

Having added the suspension pieces F F, they rested from their labors, and rejoiced in their work. Their future fame, however, was not secure; for the shrinkage of the timber, probably aided and abetted by some "old-fashioned New England snow-storms," of which we hear so much, caused the roof gradually to assume the form indicated by the dotted lines; and the natural remedy against further misplacement in that

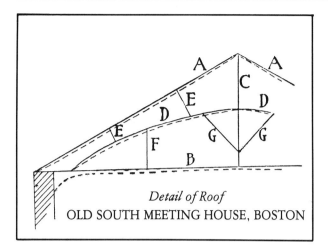

Detail of Roof
OLD SOUTH MEETING HOUSE, BOSTON

direction was the introduction of the small oak struts G G, about 3″ x 5″, which are merely notched in their thickness (3″) from one side of king-post and arched beams; showing clearly an afterthought, especially as they do not coincide in size with any of the other timbers, and are not tenoned or pinned. Then the tenons of some of the suspension pieces F broke off short; and stirrup-irons were added to make them secure.

The old roof was double-boarded, and so remains today; but at some comparatively recent period, to correct its extremely crooked condition, a new roofing was superposed upon the old, blocked up so as to make the surface true, and slated, the old covering, whether shingles or slates, being previously removed.

The ironwork is all very primitive in design and make, and speaks eloquently of the "village blacksmith," when his forge was perhaps on Park Street.

Such is something of the yarn the old roof spins; and, if the civil engineer was in those colonial days "abroad," the schoolmaster was undoubtedly in his company, as some of the appended inscriptions chalked on the old rafters would indicate:—

HOMER
April 6, 1774.
1762 February 9
A NEW ROPE FOR THE BELL.
19 POUND AND A HALF.
A NOTHER BELL ROPE
october 12, 1767.
A NOTHER BELL ROPE
August the 1, 1770.
IT WAD 20 POUND AND A HALF.
THOS. BRUCE, REPEARED THE SLEATING
May the 1st 1809.
EDWARD RUSSELL GILDED
THE FANE BALL & DIOLS
Feb. 1828.

IN the summer of 1899, owing to further deterioration of the roof-timbers and to the feeling that the building was at too much risk from fire, the old roof was replaced with one more fireproof, and Mr. Edward Atkinson has procured the accompanying view of the old framing, partly uncovered and still in place.

Such an operation as this upon such a building excited renewed archaeological interest in the building, one result of which was a letter from Mr. Abram English Brown to the Boston *Transcript*, from which we extract that portion which relates to the identifying of the till-now-unknown builder of the structure.

"The well-known historian Hamilton A. Hill, in his history of the Old South Church, has omitted but little. Yet this one fact he has failed to record, and in fact it has been hidden from all until a recent date, when an old diary was brought to light which reveals enough to settle the question so often asked.

"On a yellow page of this diary is the following: '1729, Aprell the 1st. I with others layed the foundation of the South Brick meeting house and finished the Brick work ye 8th of October, following.' On the title-page of this journal is read, '1722. Joshua Blanchard—His Book.' The conclusion is that Joshua Blanchard laid the cornerstone and built the meeting house. At that time it was customary for builders and men of prominence in an enterprise to place their initials upon cornerstones. This proved the key of the solution. Mr. Hill says: 'There is on the east side of the cornerstone "L. B. 1729," but I am not able to explain it.' He accounted for all else that had been discovered on other stones of the house. A closer inspection of the unexplained inscription developed the so-called letter 'L' into an 'I,' the lip of the 'L' proving to be a groove or defect in the stone, which, when covered from sight, leaves a perfect letter 'I.' As is well known, I and J were but one character in Latin; and in our Colonial literature were continually interchanged. It would thus seem that it had been demonstrated in two ways that Joshua Blanchard built these historic walls.

'A study of the records of the town of Boston leads us to conclude that the same man was master-builder of Faneuil Hall. It is natural enough that it should have been so, for Joshua Blanchard and Peter Faneuil were flourishing at the one time. It appears that soon after Peter Faneuil, the old Huguenot merchant, offered the gift of a market, the selectmen held a meeting of importance. 'Present the Hon. John Jeffries, Esq., Caleb Lyman, Esq., Mr. Clark, Thomas Hutchinson, Esq., and Mr. Cooke. Mr. Joshua Blanchard presented a plan from Peter Faneuil Esq., of a House for a market to be built on Dock Square (agreeable to his Proposal to the town at their meeting on Monday, the 14th of July last, and then votes thereon) Desiring the Selectmen would lay out the Ground in order to begin the foundation. The Selectmen

OLD SOUTH, BOSTON (MAY, 1899)
Showing original roof in process of demolition.

accordingly met, went on the place in order to view the Same, Mark'd and stak'd out a Piece of ground for that use, measuring in length from the lower or Easterly end, pointing the warehouse in Merchants' Row one hundred feet, and in bredth forty feet, which leaves a passageway of thirty feet wide between the Town's Shops and the market house to be built.'

"It later appears that when Faneuil Hall was completed Joshua Blanchard, acting for Peter Faneuil, presented the keys to the authorities of the town. The walls of Faneuil Hall bear added testimony to the faithful workmanship of Joshua Blanchard. They stood uninjured through the earthquake of 1756, and also through the fire of 1761, when all else of the noble structure was reduced to ashes. And, in fact, after all the changes that have taken place in that building for the century and a half of its existence. One of the sidewalks stands today as it was erected by Joshua Blanchard, an employee of Peter Faneuil, and the foundation-stones of the opposite side as it then was are the supports for some of the important pillars of the present [1899] re-building. The records of Boston further show that Joshua Blanchard was a popular mason of his time. There is little doubt that he was the builder who erected the Old Brick Meeting House that stood near the old State House, and in which many famous meetings were held during the Revolutionary Period.

"The work of the Old South and Faneuil Hall would seem a sufficient monument to the memory of this builder of Provincial Boston, but if one turns into Granary Burying-Ground and carefully examines the street corner near the Tremont Building, he will see a slab on the green sward on which we may read "No. 73. Joshua Blanchard. A Mason," and can but conclude that the ashes enclosed in that vault are all that remains of the faithful master-mason who built the walls of Old South Meeting House and Faneuil Hall."

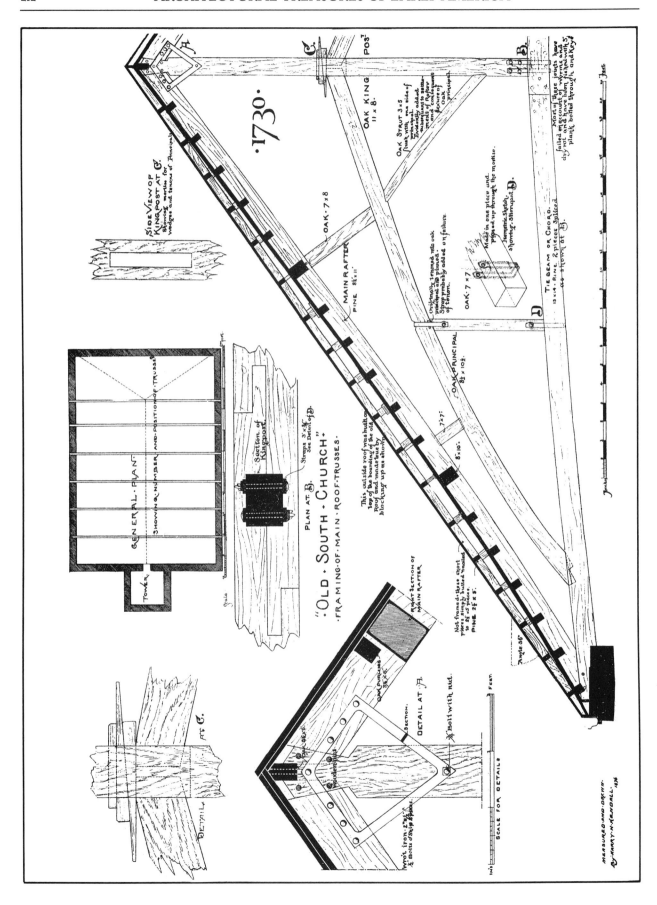

·1730·

SIDE VIEW OF KINGPOST AT C. Showing mortise for wedges and tenon of Principals

OAK KING 11 x 8.

OAK STRUT 3 x 5 fixed with one side of principal. Evidently added subsequently to settle mortise & Refrain secure of OAK principal.

POST

OAK · 7 x 8

MAIN RAFTER PINE 8¼ x11"

Originally 1 framed into oak principal as pinned. Strap probably added on failure of tenon.

Made in one piece and pinned up through the mortise. Isometric Sketch showing Strut part D.

OAK 7 x 7

TIE BEAM or CHORD. 13 x 14. PINE 2 pieces Spliced as shown at E.

"Morti" These joints here failed on account of worms and dry rot on which have taken place with 3 plank bolted through & and keyed

OAK PRINCIPAL 8¼ x 10¼

7 x 7"

8 x 10"

GENERAL · PLAN. SHOWING NUMBER AND POSITION OF TRUSSES

TOWER

Section of Kingpost

Straps 3 x ¼ See Detail of D.

PLAN AT B.

"OLD · SOUTH · CHURCH" · FRAMING · OF · MAIN · ROOF · TRUSSES ·

This outside roof was built on top the boarding of the old Roof and supported by blocking up as shown.

RIGHT SECTION OF MAIN RAFTER

Not framed these short pieces simply butted & nailed to 4 x 6 pieces. PINE 2¼ x 8"

OAK PURLINS 5¼ x 6

DETAIL AT A.

Section.

Bolt with nut.

AT C.

DETAIL

Bolt holes

Wro't Iron 2"x¼" ¾ Bolts of Ship Spikes.

SCALE FOR DETAILS

FEET.

MEASURED AND DRAWN BY HARRY · N · KENDALL 1876

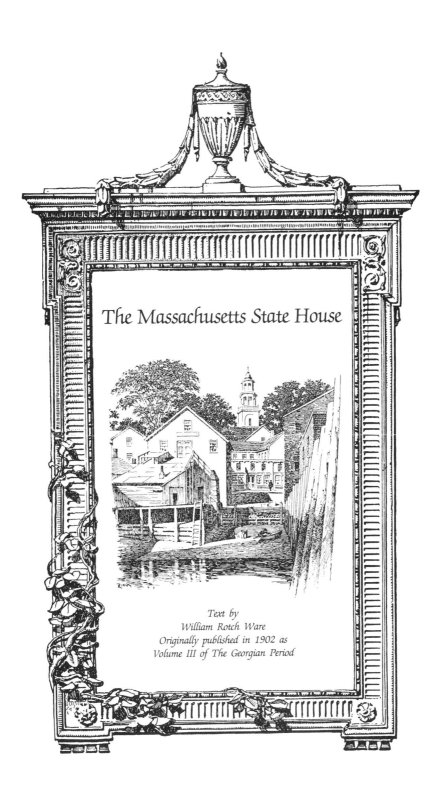

The Massachusetts State House

Text by
William Rotch Ware
Originally published in 1902 as
Volume III of The Georgian Period

OLD STATE HOUSE BOSTON
H.T. Schladermundt. DEL

THE MASSACHUSETTS STATE HOUSE, BOSTON

SINCE the attempt to do away with the "Bulfinch front" of the Massachusetts State House was the inciting cause of the publication of *The Georgian Period*, it seems proper here to give some slight indication of the character of the arguments that at last prevailed and secured the preservation of the building, and there are given below a few of the many that, at one or another of the legislative hearings, were addressed to the joint committee charged with the investigation of the question.

While the general public, not only of Boston, but of the state at large, showed a great and sustained interest in the matter, and argued the case convincedly, both pro and con, the chief factor in the fight—the discussion was often very animated, to say the least—was the Boston Society of Architects, and, more specifically, its President, Mr. Charles A. Cummings, who, in the final effort in 1895 (the question had to be debated before three several legislatures before it was finally settled in favor of the contention of the Society), was ably seconded by Mr. Clement K. Fay, a lawyer, who voluntarily charged himself with the burden and expense of conducting the case. The earlier efforts toward securing the preservation of Bulfinch's work were based mainly on architectural arguments, and though they were effective in deferring final action, it was felt wisest that at the final hearings the greatest stress should declare itself in the way of an appeal to the sentiment of the community, and preservation was finally voted as a matter of sentiment rather than because preservation was both architecturally and economically desirable.

In brief, the early history of the building is this:—

On January 30, 1795, the Legislature appointed the Hon. Edward W. Robbins, Speaker of the House, and Charles Bulfinch, architect, "to act as agents in building the State House," the most important building undertaking of the day and the first public edifice of importance to be built since the close of the Revolution. The cornerstone was laid July 4, 1795, and the Legislature opened its first session in the new building January 11, 1798. The cost of the building had been $133,333.33.

In 1853, because of the demand for more space, a large addition was built on the north [rear] side by Mr. Gridley J. F. Bryant, and in 1867 some very considerable changes in the interior of the original building were carried out by Mr. William Washburn; these consisted, in the main, of the introduction of mezzanine floors and the finishing off of rooms in the roof of the building. The changes carried out by both Bryant and Washburn were matters of record, but during the work of preservation and restoration in 1896 evidence came to light of a seemingly innumerable number of changes and alterations carried out by nameless somebodies under unrecognizable authorizations; for instance, when or by whom the original lantern crowning the dome was replaced by the one which is most familiar to living men is not known.

The work of preservation in 1896 was placed in the charge of Mr. Arthur G. Everett, of the firm Cabot, Everett & Mead, Architects, with Mr. Charles A. Cummings as consulting architect, and the work consisted, besides the strengthening of foundations and floors, of the removing of every trace of Washburn's work—Bryant's addition had already been torn down to give place to the new annex on the north—and the fireproofing of the roof and dome.

An appropriation of $375,000 was made for the restoration and fireproofing of Bulfinch's work, a sum

Corner of Council-Chamber
MASSACHUSETTS STATE HOUSE, BOSTON

which the proponents of the scheme for an entire new building declared to be wholly insufficient for the work. Mr. Everett administered his undertaking in so efficient a manner that, although $111,000 were expended upon furniture and certain work on the approaches and terraces not contemplated in the Act authorizing the expenditure, he was able to close his accounts with an unexpended balance from the original appropriation of nearly $40,000. The defenders of Bulfinch's work have been amply justified as economists, while the lesson that was given to the present and future generations as to the value of sentiment and the veneration that should be accorded to the tangible evidences of historic occurrences has been worth far more than the value of the time spent at the hearings.

If the stenographer's notes of these many hearings should be examined, abundant evidence would be found that the men of Massachusetts have, in spite of their seeming nonchalance and reserve, a warmth and delicacy of feeling that on occasion can find forceful utterance with a semblance of Gallic effusiveness. Of all the words that were spoken there were none that went more directly to the root of the matter or appealed so effectively to the conscience of each hearer than those spoken by the venerable Col. Henry Lee, who might almost be called Governor Andrew's War Secretary. Col. Lee's remarks follow the two or three

selections we have made from the interesting series of tracts that were given wide circulation during the discussions.

A CENTURY OF THE COMMONWEALTH
By Edward Everett Hole

"It will be ninety-nine years on the fourth of July since the corner-stone of what was long called the 'New State-house' was drawn to its place by fifteen white horses. The number of horses indicated the number of States in the Union; Vermont and Kentucky having been added to the old thirteen. Samuel Adams was Governor, and laid the corner-stone with due solemnity. With the next celebration of Independence, then, the hundredth year of the State-house will begin.

"It was intimated in some journal last week that the century which has passed has been so uneventful that the New State-house has no very interesting historical associations, before those connected with the War Governor and the War. It would be curious, indeed, if this were so. It would have startled George Cabot, Josiah Quincy, Elbridge Gerry, Caleb Strong, Christopher Gore, or their contemporaries, had they been told that nothing of much dramatic interest transpired in those halls in the earlier part of the century. It would have surprised Charles Bulfinch had he been told that the building he had planned had not won a place in history before it was thirty years old.

"When President Monroe visited Boston in 1817, he was, of course, officially received in the State-house by Governor Brooks. Monroe was so much pleased with the building that he asked to be introduced to Mr. Bulfinch; and it was in consequence of this visit, as it is said, that Mr. Bulfinch made the plans for the restoration of the Capitol at Washington.

"Doric Hall, the hall where the regimental colors are preserved, was familiarly called by this name during the first part of the century. It was in this hall that the meeting took place, once famous, at which Mr. Webster made his great speech in protest against the admission of Missouri. No mention will be found of this great occasion in Mr. Curtis's *Life of Webster*, because at the time he wrote that book Mr. Curtis thought it might wound the susceptibilities of the South. All the same, the meeting was held and the speech was made; and the substance of it probably remains in the address which this meeting published as the protest of Massachusetts against the extension of slavery in 1820.

"At that time the colors sent by Stark to Boston, after the Battle of Bennington, were still preserved,

End of Old Senate Chamber
MASSACHUSETTS STATE HOUSE, BOSTON
Before the restoration.

with the Hessian drum and musket, in the Senate chamber. By an unfortunate tidy turn of Mr. Messenger Kuhn, who found they were moth-eaten and dirty, the colors were destroyed in a spring cleaning under his direction. Doubtless he said that the old colors were out of repair, and that new ones would last better. Still, some of us are sorry that the eagles which the Landgrave of Hesse borrowed from Charlemagne and the Roman Empire did not escape the hand of modern repair and improvement. We lost the chance then to say: —

> 'So even Roman banners fall
> To hide the time-stains on our wall.'

"The Commissioners now tell us about the whole building what Mr. Kuhn said about the banners; it is old and out of repair, and a new one can be had for money, and the State is rich.

"The State conventions of 1820 and 1853 were both held in this State-house. The wealth of oratory and of wisdom, from all men of mark, was lavished here. Men sat in those bodies who had never served in the General Court, in their readiness to help in framing permanent institutions of the Commonwealth. Webster, Story, most of the judges of our own courts, indeed, have sooner or later taken part in the deliberations here. In 1853, Sumner and Phillips, neither of whom ever sat in the Legislature, were in the convention. In State Legislatures and public hearings I have heard Charles Francis Adams, Benjamin Franklin, Thomas Peleg Sprague, Francis Wayland, Edward Everett, and many others, orators or statesmen; some of them in the days when the State-house was not half a century old.

"Every European traveller of distinction, who had any claim to be presented to the Governor of his time, was taken, of course, to the State-house. It would be fair to say that, with its wealth of archives, the two charters, the statue of Washington, the relics of the older monument, it represented the Commonwealth as no single man could do. Lafayette was received here in 1824; a few years later General Jackson was received here. The ceremony was the more distinguished because the hosts supposed his advent to the presidency to be a permanent injury to the Constitution; and they were obliged to show, in every detail of their hospitality, that they were Americans and gentlemen, though they did not 'Hurrah for Jackson.' Princes of every grade, from Keokuk and Blackhawk round to the Prince of Wales and Prince Alexis, have been received here. It was after an hour in the Governor's room, where the Earl of Ellesmere, the Governor of Canada, had seen Andrew's ministrations in their detail, that he thanked the Governor for his hospitality and said, 'I understand your institutions as I never did before.'

"Indeed, it was the work of the War, with the great War Governor and the loyal staff who served him so well using every inch of the State-house for the duty which Massachusetts had in that crisis, it was this, more than everything else, which has endeared the old New State-house to this generation."

THE CROWN OF BEACON HILL
BY CHARLES A. CUMMINGS

"There are signs that the people are waking up to the danger which threatens the State-house on Beacon Hill. They must do more than wake up, if they wish to save it. The impression has become general, the press has lately fostered it, that its destruction is a matter of necessity; that its foundations are weak, its woodwork

End of Old Senate Chamber
MASSACHUSETTS STATE HOUSE, BOSTON
Before the restoration.

Before Restoration (1895)
MASSACHUSETTS STATE HOUSE—1798—BOSTON, MASSACHUSETTS
Charles Bulfinch, Architect

decayed, and its general condition unsafe and threatening ruin.

"It is very necessary to say with emphasis that this is an entirely false impression, and that among the various parties directly interested in replacing the present building by a new and more ambitious structure not one has claimed that there is any weakness or failure in any part of the State-house except in the dome. The dome is a small hemisphere about 50 feet in diameter, of which the framing is of pine joists or planks, considerably lighter, no doubt, than we should use to-day in a similar work, and which rests on two wooden trusses. These trusses have been carried down at one extremity by the weight (as is understood) of a large water-tank which was put in at the time the elevator was introduced. It is also doubtless true that the framing-timbers just spoken of have suffered more or less from dry-rot and ravages of worms. But the replacing of these timbers with sound ones of greater size, and the blocking up of the dome to its true level, is a trifling matter, involving (as one of the Commissioners admits) no difficulty and small expense, and could be done without any interference with the daily use of the building below.

It is true, further, that the interior disposition of the wings at the ends of the building as executed by Bulfinch was changed in the lowest story during the tasteless and unskillful alterations made some thirty years ago, under the direction of Mr. Washburn, by the insertion of an intermediate floor, which divided the ample chambers of Mr. Bulfinch in order to give the Legislature some necessary committee-rooms, but which greatly detracted from the propriety and dignity of that portion of the interior. These additional rooms have now been rendered unnecessary by the ample provision made by Mr. Brigham in the extension buildings, now nearly completed, and nothing prevents the removal of the intermediate floors and the restoration of the wings to their original condition.

"But all this has really very little to do with the case as it now stands. If the Commissioners wished to retain the present building, there would be nothing heard of its bad condition. They would go to work quietly where they found repairs needed and put it in a good and safe condition. They do *not* wish to retain it. It is very old, they say; it is a hundred years old; it cannot stand much longer; better take it down now while we are concerned with it, and have something new and more in accordance with what we are just finishing behind it.

After Restoration (1897)
MASSACHUSETTS STATE HOUSE — 1798 — BOSTON, MASSACHUSETTS
Charles Bulfinch, Architect

"Well, it is not to be doubted that their new building would be in many respects of construction better and safer than the old one. It would certainly be more splendid, and more in accordance with modern methods. But is that the only consideration?

"We say, No, nor yet the chief consideration. What is most valuable is the State-house of a hundred years ago, its history: its associations with the men of other days, the inexpressible, undefinable flavor of earlier times when life was simpler and when the name of Massachusetts stood for all that was noble and fine in citizenship, can never be transferred to a new State-house. Add to this, which is a consideration rightly enough characterized as "sentimental," the simple, noble and dignified aspect of the building and the extreme improbability that any more ambitious successor will ever possess these qualities in equal measure, and we are justified, I think, in saying that the destruction of the State-house would be a lamentable concession to the modern American spirit which carries us every year farther away from the 'nobler modes of life, with sweeter manners, purer laws,' which our fathers knew, the spirit of false progress, false ambition, false pride."

This series of tracts was admirably effective, but as

they lacked the emphasis of vocal inflection and did not afford ocular proof of the sincerity and earnestness of the protestant they did not have the force and effectiveness of the words personally addressed to the joint committee by many distinguished and humble citizens alike. It was a real intellectual treat to attend those hearings. But of all the words that were uttered none, probably, were quite so impressive as Colonel Lee's.

REMARKS OF COL. HENRY LEE

"This is a matter of sentiment, as Governor Rice said. He who does not value sentiment ought not to be here. John Winthrop valued sentiment, or he would not have come here; so did his companions. They had nothing but sentiment and piety to preserve them and keep their courage up, as had the Plymouth Fathers. It seems to be rather late in the day for us of Massachusetts to abandon sentiment. It has money value as well as its moral value. When I first remember Boston, it was filled with sentiment. The buildings, which stood mostly apart with their gardens, were Provincial, some of them going back to Colonial times. As the city grew — as the town grew, for it was not a city then — as the town grew and room was wanted for the population, these old buildings came down gradually and gave way to blocks of buildings; but many of them might have been preserved, and in looking back, we see that if the sentiment of the time had inspired people to their preservation, there would have been money value in it. There stood the old Province House, a proud old building, one of the few remains of Colonial magnificence, built in 1679 by Peter Sargent, for many years the vice-regal court of this Province, the abode of nine Provincial Governors, one after another, from a testy old Colonel of Marlborough's army down to Sir William Howe, who left it at the time of the evacuation of Boston. That might have stood behind its oak-trees on its terraces, a grand, stately old building, and would have been much handsomer, in my opinion, than our new City-hall—I suppose Mr.—[1] would have preferred the new City-hall; I don't. There was Sir William Phips's house, that old buccaneer, to fulfil the dreams of his boyhood; and when I was a boy, it was used as the Boys' Asylum: that stood down on Charter Street, a grand old building. There was the house of Governor Hutchinson and his father, which house was so fine that, after Hutchinson was made Governor, he said he didn't want to go and live in the Province House, because he had a better one down at the North End; that and the house of Sir Harry Frankland stood side by side in Garden Court Street. That house I have seen in my boyhood, and am one of the few now living who ever saw it, a most remarkable specimen of Provincial architecture; but pulled down ruthlessly. It would have been well to have preserved it. There was the beautiful Hancock house, well remembered; and Governor Andrew did all that he could to preserve it. It would have been most appropriate for the official residence of the Governor of Massachusetts, and could have been bought for less than you paid for an ordinary house on the other side of the way a few years afterwards; and there, sentiment, if it had ruled the hour, would have been found in the end to have been profitable. There were long lines of houses: all Pemberton Hill was covered with them; Peter Faneuil's house, the giver of the hall; there was the house of Sir Harry Vane, afterwards Rev. John Cotton's house; there was Governor Bellingham's house; and these with their grounds would have made a beautiful park for the city, and we should not have had to go out five or six miles to find our park. It would have been well to have preserved them.

"There were fortifications. Some one spoke here as if there had never been any associations in this country,

ex-Senator—, no other associations but the Revolutionary associations. I think there have been a great many associations, but if you come to Revolutionary associations, there was the fortification on the Common that was levelled when I was in College; there were the fortifications at the South End; there were the fortifications on Mystic River, where afterwards the convent was built, and a cordon of earthworks from Mystic River through Somerville, Cambridge, Brookline, Roxbury, ending with Dorchester Heights; memorials of the Siege of Boston and of Washington's trials. And I think a beautiful parkway could have been made and these fortifications preserved for a very small amount of money, and sentiment would have been found to have been economy in the end. But those were the interesting monuments of my boyhood and youth.

"A monument, what is a monument? There were some rich men who thought a monument ought to be something new; they had Mr.—'s idea about it, that it ought to be something new, something in the present style. I don't know whether the dome of St. Peter's had been changed to the modern style to attract people or not! They thought this monument ought to be something new, something pretty fine, finer than the earthworks which were there. When my father took me over to see Bunker Hill, there were the earthworks; one could see the redoubt on which Prescott stood; see the breastwork; see where the rail fence ran. One could see all the way down to the Navy Yard, to Moulton's Point, where the British landed. That was something like a monument; it was not a mere *record*, which the Monument afterwards was; it was a *reminder* of the scene, and that is what a monument should be. You stood there, and all the sentiment of the battle came to you. Now, you go there, and you stand upon a hill, nicely graded and all the redoubt and breastwork filled up and erased, and you have the pleasure of seeing an Egyptian obelisk! Well, it is a matter of taste: to me the old earthworks would have been more inspiring, more suggestive, without the Egyptian obelisk. Mr.— has a different mind. It is a free country; we all have a right to our opinion.

"If you want to save the State-house, you want to save it as a matter of sentiment: it is easier now that they have built that remarkably exaggerated building behind.

"During the war, when Governor Andrew worked night and day, when war as well as peace was carried on, the State-house was sufficiently large. What they want a building seven times as large for, I don't know, unless every legislator is seven times as big as he was in those days. I was to-day guided through; I went to the farther end. I was told you were to be in No. 29. Then

---

[1] A previous speaker, who favored the demolition of the State House.

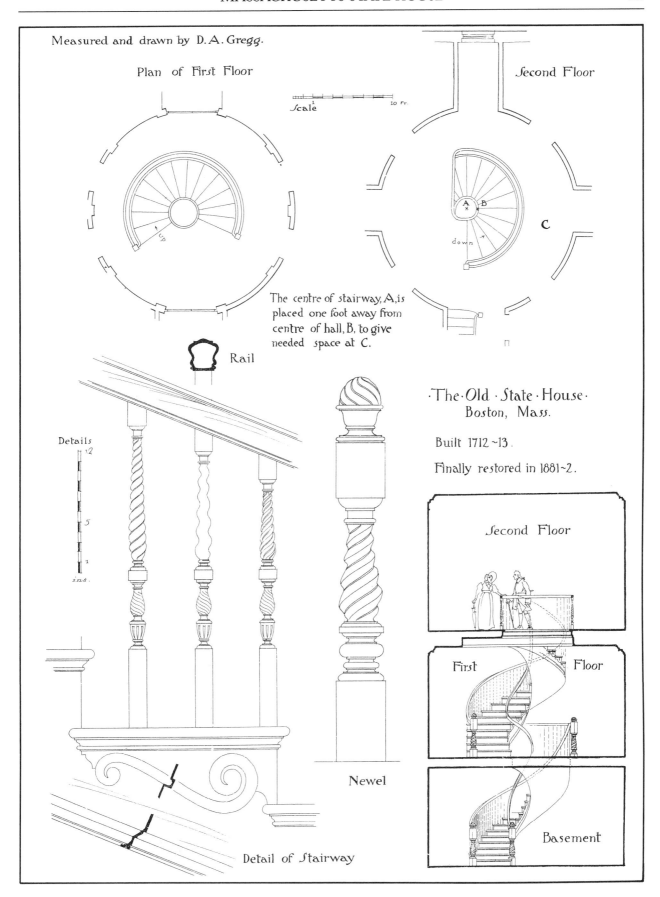

Measured and drawn by D.A. Gregg.

Plan of First Floor

Scale   10 Fr.

Second Floor

The centre of stairway, A, is placed one foot away from centre of hall, B, to give needed space at C.

Rail

Details

·The·Old·State·House·
Boston, Mass.

Built 1712~13.

Finally restored in 1881~2.

Second Floor

First   Floor

Basement

Newel

Detail of Stairway

I came to No. 8. I could not come without a guide. What you want such a building for, I don't know; but it is built. I suppose you want it, as Mr.— says, to advertise the State; or it was wanted for some other purpose. Well, I think it is a great pity.

"A great many years ago, my father bought a house in Brookline. It was an historic house; it was, part of it, 230 years old. In that house had been born Susannah Boylston, the mother of John Adams, the first John Adams. I have a letter of John Adams's, saying that he has not been there since he was a youth and brought his mother on horseback on a pillion behind him. The carpenter told me when I wanted him to make some repairs for my father, 'I tell you, Mr. Lee, the cheapest thing you can do is to pull that house right down.' He found that there was some dry-rot in it, that there were some of the studs worn off at the bottom, and some other things; and that carpenter was of Mr.——'s opinion, that a new house was wanted; that it would *advertise* my father better than the old house. And I did not do it; I kept the old house in spite of its being "powder-posted"; I have kept it, it is now forty years, and I can say that I never go to that house, for I don't live in it, one of my sons lives in it, I never go to that house without an active sensation of pleasure. Why? Well, when you go aboard, what do you go to see? Do you go to see the *new* houses in London? Do you go to see the new Law Courts? Do you go to see that griffin that they put up where Temple Bar stood? No, you go at once, the minute you can dust your clothes, out you go to see Westminster Abbey. I have no doubt there is rot in Westminster Abbey. I have no doubt some stones have crumbled, and I think it *would* advertise London if they built a new one. But what should you think when you came to London and asked for Westminster Abbey and they should say, 'Well, you can't see the Abbey, but you can see a model of the Abbey; it was thought in the way and that we ought to have something new, something to *advertise* London, and we have taken down the Abbey'?

"Now, is it healthy? Perhaps that is one reason they took it down: took it down because it was too old and too much dry-rot in it, and they wanted something new, something up to the times, Mr.——. And the Tower, 'Well, yes, you can see the Tower, but who wants to go and see the Tower'? Why, you do, the American, who is going to pull down the State-house. You go abroad on purpose to see the Temple, the Tower and the Abbey and all the antiquities that you can find in London, not looking at anything else.

"Then some say this State-house is only a hundred years old. Governor Long found that out last year; only a hundred years old? Well, I have seen the Abbey and I have seen the Temples of Paestum, and Augus-

tus Caesar stood and looked at them and knew no more about who built them than I do; but his feeling of antiquity and association was just the same as mine when looking at the Abbey.

"You want a reminder if you come to the State-house. You don't want a new building to recall that here was the old State-house once, built by Bulfinch, and which had witnessed the first hundred years of the history of the State. It is all the history there is. Governor Long doesn't seem to think there is any history. Now, he has been one of the Governors; there have been thirty-five Governors since this building was built, and they have all been good Governors, and it is hardly to be supposed that there is *no* record, that we have had *no* history all these hundred years. There have been many interesting events. He said there had been no war, excepting the War of the Rebellion. That was rather a mistake: we had the War of 1812, which was a very distressing war, too; it robbed us of most of our property and was one that we were very averse to. We had the victories of 1812. Up through the streets marched Commodore Hull and Captain Dacre. They lived together in the Exchange Coffee-house, and came to the State-house to pay their respects to the Governor. There was the fight between the '*Chesapeake*' and '*Shannon*'; the women were witnessing from the dome with anxious eyes that terrible defeat.

"There were many events I remember: the coming of Lafayette in 1824, who was received here, as he was the next year, when he came to the laying of the corner-stone of the Bunker Hill Monument; that is something of an event. President Monroe came here in 1817; that was something of an event. There have been four or five presidents here since then.

"We come down to the Civil War. Why, he said, Governor Andrew—yes, he believed there was a war—but he thought Governor Andrew was on the steps; it was not *in* the State-house; he was on the steps; he gave the flags and he took the flags on the steps. Well, if you should be inclined to save your father's house and somebody should say to you, 'Why, I saw your father bid you good-bye in the stage-coach on the steps.' Yes, but I saw my father in the house, too. There was something done in the State-house in those long, tearful years of agony and weariness, heart-breaking, disappointment and losses; the procession of young men coming to offer themselves for service, saluting the Governor, like the gladiators the Emperor, 'We who are about to die salute you.'

Do you suppose there is no feeling connected with the rooms where the Governor sat for those four years? a man of peace called upon suddenly to prepare this State for a fearful war, and preparing it in spite of ridicule, in spite of denunciation, and preparing it so

Old Senate Chamber · Massachusetts State House · Boston ·
Charles Bulfinch Architect ·
[1798]

· Measured and drawn by E·P·Morrill ·

·plaster·

·wood·

promptly that Massachusetts was the first State: the first men who were sent properly equipped and armed for the war were the men of Massachusetts. The whole world wept for Lincoln's death; are there no tears for Andrew, who fell, after the war, as much as Lincoln? He was killed by an assassin, but if he had not been, he would have died in a short time from head and heart weariness. Do you suppose Governor Andrew could have sat here those four years, night and day, for he was here much of the time night and day, working and enduring, and feeling that he had been, more or less, instrumental in bringing about the deaths of all the flower of Massachusetts, without any emotions? Was there no association? You have the association with Bunker Hill—for what? A battle of four hours. Has a battle of four years no association for this building, the agony of those four years? Men, haggard with anxiety and grief, and the mourners going about the streets from every house; Rachel weeping for her children and would not be comforted because they were not. Is there no association for this building, where the headquarters of the whole Government of the time were? It seems to me absurd.

"I should like to read a small sentence from William Morris, on this subject: 'No man who consents to the destruction of an ancient building has any right to pretend that he cares about art; or has any excuse to plead in defence of his crime against civilization and progress save sheer brutal ignorance.'

"Now I have only one word more to say. In 1870 the Commune in Paris pulled down the Tuileries. I was there the next year; I saw the destruction. They pulled down the column on the Place Vendôme, of which they had been so proud. Now the whole of France is all alive with admiration for Napoleon. They destroyed the Hôtel de Ville with its priceless treasures. What was it? The work of brutes. Now we are proposing to destroy not our Hôtel de Ville, but our State-house, and do it deliberately, in cold blood. If any of you should be hauled up for killing a person, the judge would make a distinction whether you did it in hot blood, whether you did it under provocation, or whether you did it in cold blood. If you did it in cold blood, he will hang you; if you did it in hot blood, he will let you off with imprisonment for life. So, we are to be more brutal, more culpable than those brutish Parisians who destroyed their monuments! We do it in cold blood. In this case, there is no excuse; you are doing it in cold blood."

The battle that was waged in Massachusetts over the Bulfinch front of the State House finds an echo in the contest which is at this moment going on over the retention or the destruction of the present City Hall[2] in Hartford, Connecticut. Curiously enough, this former State House is by some said to be also the work of Charles Bulfinch—and the cupola looks as if it might have been designed by Bulfinch, but if this is so it is curious that it is not mentioned in the autographic list of his buildings which was found amongst Bulfinch's papers. But whoever was the architect, the building, erected in 1796, is an interesting one, and as the Connecticut Historical Society, the Daughters of the Revolution and kindred societies are making the same sort of appeal to the sentiment of the community that eventually proved successful in Boston, and have already secured a sort of stay of proceedings, it may be hoped with some degree of confidence that the ultimate outcome of the agitation will rank the chief city of Connecticut alongside of the metropolis of New England as communities where the intellectual rights of civilization are respected, and success here will encourage similar effort in the case of valued "monuments" elsewhere.

ENVOI

IN bringing to an end his enjoyable connection with this work the editor feels obliged to confess to a regret that so important an undertaking could not have fallen to the share of someone who, besides being better fitted for the task, might have had at command both the necessary time and the equally needful capital to do thoroughly and well what has been done so imperfectly.

It is "a thousand pities" that when architects began, twenty years [1882] or so ago, to turn their attention again to the possibilities that lie in the Georgian style—when it is used with discretion and refinement—there was not in existence some such comprehensive work as this. For the lack of it and through the imperfect understanding of the style which naturally grew out of this lack the country has been endowed with a vast quantity of buildings, intended to express the spirit of "Old Colonial" work, which, because of their ill-considered proportions and vulgar overdressing with applied ornament, are too often mere caricatures of the style.

On the other hand, it is doubtful whether such a work as this could have been brought out much earlier. In a large measure it results from the following up of clues afforded by the chance observation of the ever-wandering amateur photographer, whose name is legion and whose footsteps cover every portion of the country. A score of years ago the "Kodak" and the amateur photographer were not, and all that the architect had for his guidance were such notes as he could make and such inferences as he could draw from the comparatively few examples of good work that could be found in his immediate neighborhood.

We are profoundly grateful for the large amount of assistance we have had in the way of written data, loaned photographs and drawings of measured work voluntarily placed at our service, without demand for compensation, by many different individuals.

To select for special expression of gratitude any of these appreciated coöperators is somewhat invidious, but we feel that we ought to make special acknowledgment of the kindness of the officials of the Massachusetts Institute of Technology, who placed at our service the measured drawings made by the students in their Summer School of Architecture—which acknowledgment equally signalizes our appreciation of the intelligent activity of the students who did the actual work. But beyond this, thanks are due to Mrs. Thaddeus Horton, who not only has contributed several interesting papers on Southern work and has placed at our service a large collection of photographs of Southern buildings, but has also secured valuable material through the use of her own camera.

WM. ROTCH WARE

---

[2] TOWNE, ITHIEL—Born in 1784. Died, 1844. In partnership with A. J. Davis he built the State House at New Haven, and later in his career he designed the (old) State House of Indiana and the North Carolina State House. The City Hall (not the old State House) in Hartford, Connecticut, was also his work, and some of the Government buildings at Washington were built after his designs. He built many houses and churches in the Connecticut Valley, from Northampton to New Haven, and also in New York State.

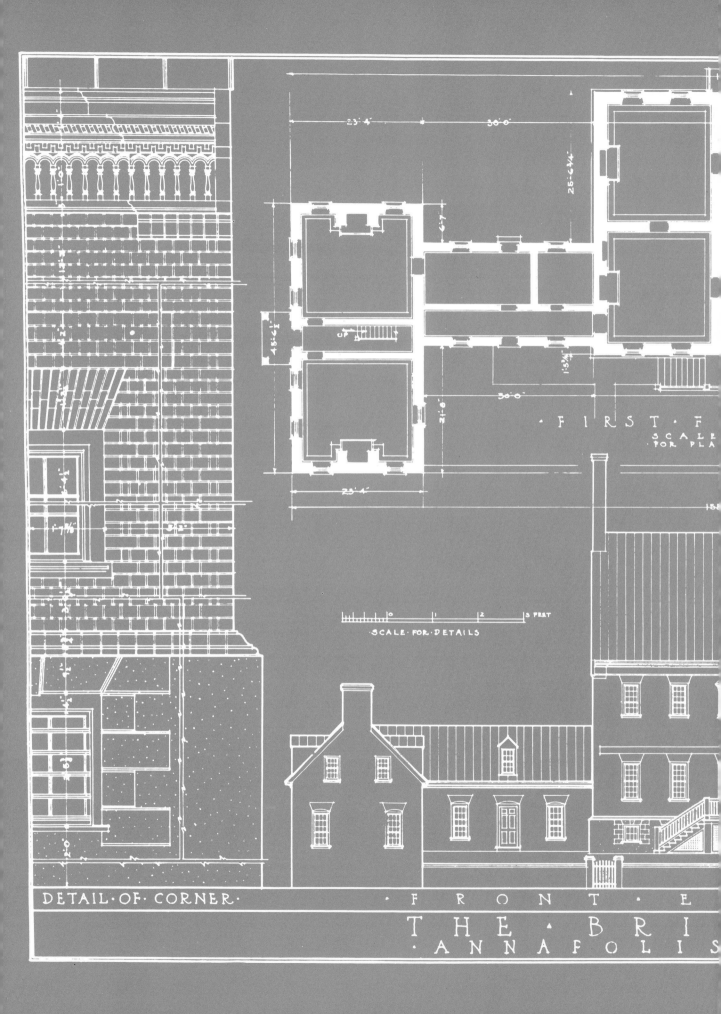

DETAIL·OF·CORNER·

·F R O N T · E

·FIRST·F
SCALE
FOR PLA

SCALE·FOR·DETAILS

T H E · B R I

·A N N A P O L I S

36'-0"

23'-4"

26'-6¼"